You can Write Song Lyrics

Terry Cox

WRITER'S DIGEST BOOKS
CINCINNATI, OHIO
www.writersdigest.com

You Can Write Song Lyrics. Copyright © 2000 by Terry Cox. Manufactured in the United States of America. All rights reserved. No part of this book may be reproduced in any form or by any electronic or mechanical means including information storage and retrieval systems without permission in writing from the publisher, except by a reviewer, who may quote brief passages in a review. Published by Writer's Digest Books, an imprint of F&W Publications, Inc., 4700 East Galbraith Road, Cincinnati, Ohio 45236. (800) 289-0963. First edition.

Visit our Web site at www.writersdigest.com for information on more resources for writers.

To receive a free weekly e-mail newsletter delivering tips and updates about writing and about Writer's Digest products, send an e-mail with "Subscribe Newsletter" in the body of the message to newsletter-request@writersdigest.com, or register directly at our Web site at www.writersdigest.com.

08   07   06   05   04   7   6   5   4   3

Library of Congress Cataloging-in-Publication Data

Cox, Terry
   You can write song lyrics / by Terry Cox.
      p.   cm.
   Includes index.
   ISBN 0-89879-989-9 (pbk.)
      1. Lyric writing (Popular music) 2. Popular music—Writing and publishing.
   I. Title.

MT67.C68   2000
782.42164ft0268—dc21   00-040851
                                                                       CIP

Editor: David Borcherding
Cover designed by: Wendy Dunning
Cover photography by: Hale Photography, Inc.
Production coordinator: Mark Griffin
Author photo: Gittel Price

Permissions on the next two pages constitute an extension of this copyright page.
Cover photo shot on location at Group Effort Sound Studios, Crescent Springs, KY.

Whole or partial lyrics of the following songs are reprinted in this book and used with permission from corresponding publishers, all rights reserved. This page constitutes an extension of the copyright page.

"Anywhere Is Paradise" (Stefan Andersson/Terry Cox)
© 1996 BMG Music Publishing Scandinavia AB (STIM)/Fisher Queen Songs, aka Fisher King Songs (Admin. by Careers BMG Music Publishing Inc. for U.S. & Canada) (BMI)

"Back At One" (Brian McKnight)
© 1999 Cancelled Lunch Music/Universal-Polygram Int'l Publishing, Inc. (ASCAP)

"Belly-Up Blues" (Louise Hoffsten/Terry Cox)
© 1996 Courtstone Music and BMG Music Publishing Scandinavia AB (STIM)/ Fisher Queen Songs (Admin. by BMG Songs, Inc. for U.S. & Canada) (ASCAP)

"Eternal Flame" (Susanna Hoffs/Tom Kelly/Billy Steinberg)
© 1988 Sony/ATV Tunes LLC (BMI) /EMI Blackwood Music Inc. and Bangophile Music (BMI)

"Every December Sky" (Beth Nielsen Chapman)
© 1999 Almo Music Corp. and BNC Songs (Lic. by Warner Bros. Publications U.S. Inc.) (ASCAP)

"Goodbye Earl" (Dennis Linde)
© 1999 EMI Blackwood Music Inc. (BMI)

"Hole In My Head" (Buddy Miller/Jim Lauderdale)
© 1997 Martha Road Music and Tinkie Tunes (Admin. by Bug Music Corp.) (ASCAP)/Laudersongs and Mighty Nice Music (Admin. by Bluewater Music Corp.) (BMI)

"I Don't Want to Miss a Thing" (Diane Warren)
© 1998 RealSongs (Lic. by Warner Bros. Publications U.S. Inc.) (ASCAP)

"If I Fall You're Going Down With Me" (Matraca Berg/Annie Roboff)
© 1999 Hillbillith Music/Songs Of Sally Sue's Medicine Show/Songs of Universal (div. of Universal Studios) (BMI)/Almo Music Corp. and Anwa Music (Lic. by Warner Bros. Publications U.S. Inc.) (ASCAP)

"If It Makes You Happy" (Sheryl Crow/Jeffrey Trott)
© 1996 Warner-Tamerlane Publishing Co./Old Crow Music (Admin. by Warner-Tamerlane)/Trottsky Music (Admin. by Wixen Music Publishing Co.) (BMI) (Lic. by Warner Bros. Publications U.S. Inc.)

"Just Enough Rope" (Michael Lunn/Mike Noble)
© 1998 WB Music Corp. and Lunn Music (ASCAP)/Warner-Tamerlane Publishing Corp. and Under the Bridge Music (BMI) (Lic. by Warner Bros. Publications U.S. Inc.)

"Last Kiss "(Wayne Cochran)
©) 1961, 1964 (Renewed) Fort Knox Music Inc./Trio Music Company. Inc. (BMI).

"Let Me Love You One More Time" (Michael Peterson/John Bettis)
© 1999 Fixed Points Music (Admin by Warner-Tamerlane Publishing Corp.) BMI/Words by John (Admin. by WB Music Corp.) (ASCAP) (Lic. by Warner Bros. Publications U.S. Inc.)

"Love is All" (Arnie Roman)
(c) 1999 Romanesque Music/Annotation Music (Admin by WB Music Corp.) (ASCAP) (Lic. by Warner Bros. Publications U.S. Inc.)

"Love is on the Way" (Peter Zizzo/Denise Rich/Tina Shafer)
© 1996 Pez Music/Connotation Music/Dream IDG Publishing (Admin. War-

ner-Tamerlane Publ. Corp.) (Lic. by Warner Bros. Publications U.S. Inc.)
(BMI)/Ensign Music and Tinabird Music (BMI)/Duffield Corporation (Admin.
by SONY-ATV Music Publishing Canada).

"My Heart Will Go On" (James Horner/Will Jennings)
© 1997 Famous Music Corporation and Ensign Music Corporation (ASCAP)/
Fox Film Music Corp./TCF Music Inc./Blue Sky Rider Songs (Admin. by Irving
Music, Inc.) (Lic. by Warner Bros. Publications U.S. Inc.) (BMI)

"Nobody's Supposed to Be Here" (Montell Jordan/Anthony "Shep" Crawford)
© 1998 Famous Music Corporation (ASCAP) and Almo Music Corp./Hudson
Jordan Music/Shep & Shep Publishing (Admin. by Almo Music Corp.) (Lic.
by Warner Bros. Publications U.S. Inc.) (ASCAP)

"One Of Us" (Eric Bazilian)
© 1995, 1996 Human Boy Music (Admin. by WB Music Corp (Lic. by Warner
Bros. Publications U.S. Inc.) (ASCAP)

"The River" (Victoria Shaw/Garth Brooks)
© 1991 Gary Morris Music (Admin. by BMG Songs, Inc.) (ASCAP)/Major
Bob Music Co., Inc. and Mid-Summer Music Co., Inc. (Lic. by Warner Bros.
Publications U.S. Inc.) (ASCAP)

"The Secret of Life" (Gretchen Peters)
© 1994 Sony/ATV Tunes LLC and Purple Crayon Music (Admin. by Sony/ATV
Music Publishing)

"Sheeps' Clothing" (Stefan Andersson/Terry Cox)
© 1996 BMG Music Publishing Scandinavia AB (STIM)/Fisher Queen Songs,
aka Fisher King Songs (Admin. by Careers BMG Music Publishing Inc. for
U.S. & Canada) (BMI)

"Sometimes" (Jorgen Elofsson)
© 1999 Grantsville Publishing Ltd. (Admin. by Zomba Enterprises Inc. for
U.S. & Canada) BMG Music Publishing Scandinavia AB (Admin. in U.S. by
BMG Songs, Inc.) (STIM) (Lic. by Warner Bros. Publications U.S. Inc.)

"The Song Remembers When "(Hugh Prestwood)
© 1993 Careers-BMG Music Publishing and Hugh Prestwood Music (BMI)

"Standing Outside the Fire" (Garth Brooks/Jenny Yates)
© 1993 Criterion Music Corp. & Escudilla Music (ASCAP)/Major Bob Music
Co., Inc. & No Fences Music (Admin. by Major Bob Music Co., Inc. (Lic. by
Warner Bros. Publications U.S. Inc.) (ASCAP)

"This Kiss" (Robin Lerner/Annie Roboff/Beth Nielsen Chapman)
© 1998 Puckalesia Songs/Nomad-Noman Music & Warner-Tamerlane Pub.
Corp. (BMI)/Almo Music Corp. and Anwa Music (ASCAP)/Almo Music Corp.
& BNC Songs (ASCAP) (Lic. by Warner Bros. Publications U.S. Inc.)

"Through Your Hands" (John Hiatt)
© 1996 Careers-BMG Music Publishing and Whistling Moon Traveler (BMI)

"Torn" (Scott Cutler/Anne Preven/ Phil Thornalley)
© 1995, 1996 Phil Thornalley Music and BMG Music Pub. Ltd (Admin. by
BMG Songs, Inc.) (ASCAP)/ Universal-Songs Of Polygram Int'l and Weetie Pie
Music (BMI)/Colgems EMI Music Inc. and Scott Cutler Music (ASCAP)

"True Colors" (Tom Kelly/Billy Steinberg)
© 1986 Sony/ATV Tunes LLC. (Admin. by Sony/ATV Music Publishing)
(ASCAP)

"Unbreak My Heart" (Diane Warren)
© 1996 RealSongs (Lic. by Warner Bros. Publications U.S. Inc.) (ASCAP)

"Under a Low-Ceilinged Sky "(Stefan Andersson/Terry Cox)
© 1996 BMG Music Publishing Scandinavia AB (STIM)/Fisher Queen Songs,
aka Fisher King Songs (Admin. by Careers BMG Music Publishing Inc. for
U.S. & Canada) (BMI)

 Terry Cox is a lyric writer who has co-written over 150 songs for CDs, film and TV for artists such as Vanessa Williams, Patti Austin, Grover Washington Jr., David Broza, Clay Crosse, Louise Hoffsten, Meja and many others. Film credits include an end title song performed by Swedish artist Robyn for "On the Line" starring Lance from 'N Sync, Steve Martin's *Roxanne*, and various foreign films. TV performances of songs include PopStars, *Baywatch*, *Disney*, *The Early Show*, *Conan O'Brien*, *Arsenio Hall*, *One Life to Live*, *Another World*, *All My Children* and Sweden's Skilda Varldar, as well as songs and jingles for HBO, Burger King, Toshiba, Tyson Foods, Swiffer and others. She has also co-written songs for special projects such as "Broadway Cares," a CD recorded in the grotto birthplace of Jesus entitled "Christmas in Bethlehem" featuring Swedish artist Carola and multi-national guest artists, and a performance by Israeli megastar David Broza at the 1995 Rabin memorials in Madison Square Garden and Washington, D.C.

Terry has been a staff writer with Columbia Pictures, Filmtrax and BMG Music, and her own music publishing company, Fisher Queen Songs, is currently affiliated in Europe with Warner-Chappell, BMG and others. She has worked extensively in the Swedish pop music scene, and her travels have given her a diverse experience in mainstream and alternative pop, rock, country, R&B, folk, jazz, Celtic, gospel and world music, including translations and adaptations of Spanish, French, Italian, Scandinavian and Hebrew songs and poems. In addition, she mentors private students and conducts group workshops on the "magic and mechanics" of lyric/songwriting, poetry and prose, as well as consulting for music publishing, songplugging, song contracts and other aspects of the music business. She has been a guest speaker for schools, churches and other organizations on a variety of subjects that include writing as a way of accessing knowledge and the transformative mix of creativity, spirituality and consciousness.

In addition to ongoing songwriting and mentoring, she's always at work on "that next book"—and when she's not on the road, she lives on a hill in Cold Spring, New York. See www.fisherqueensongs.com for a current discography and information on workshops and other activities.

ACKNOWLEDGMENTS

This book would not have been possible without the help of so many! I am especially grateful to the following songwriters and artists for baring your creative souls and reminding me of the heart that keeps us all going: Billy Steinberg, Annie Roboff, Arnie Roman, Tanya Leah, John Bettis, Peter Zizzo, Tina Shafer, Eric Bazilian, Steve Dorff, Hugh Prestwood, George Green, Beth Nielsen Chapman, Jenny Yates, Bette Sussman, Kathy Sommer, Alex Forbes, Shelley Peiken, Warren and Tamara Hill, Robert Sterling, Louise Hoffsten, Meja, Jade, Jorgen Elofsson, Tommy Ekman and Andreas Carlsson. Thank you for your words of wisdom and for the great lyrics that some of you contributed to this book. I'm also grateful to all the licensor VIPs for additional lyric contributions from the songs of John Hiatt, Diane Warren, James Horner, Will Jennings, Sheryl Crow, Jeffrey Trott, Brian McKnight, Susanna Hoffs, Tom Kelly, Dennis Linde, Buddy Miller, Jim Lauderdale, Matraca Berg, Gretchen Peters, Michael Lunn, Mike Noble, Michael Peterson, Wayne Cochran, Denise Rich, Garth Brooks, Victoria Shaw, Robin Lerner, Scott Cutler, Anne Preven, Phil Thornalley, Montell Jordan, Anthony Crawford and Stefan Andersson.

I also want to thank those who so generously consulted with me on the content of the book: Arnie Roman, Peter Zizzo, Art Labriola, Billy Steinberg, Jenny Yates, Kathy Sommer, Cindy Cox, Amy Lee, ASCAP's Marcie Drexler and Cindy Collins, BMI's Antonella DiSaverio, Gary Roth, Charlie Feldman and Del Bryant, Bob Leone of the Songwriters Hall of Fame, George Wurzbach of the Songwriters Guild, Pat Pattison of the Berklee College of Music, Vince DeGiorgio and Dave Novik of RCA Records, Lee Hubner of Sony Music and Evan Lamberg and Bruce Burch of EMI Music Publishing.

Special thanks to goddaughter Lindy Labriola, who gave me good heart-food hugs when I needed extra energy; Libby Healy, for magnificent shelter; Harriet and Ken Appleman, for their never-ending love and concern; and to my assistant Hannah Campbell, for putting up with the pace and being such an enthusiastic song consultant all the way to the last note. And to my editor Dave Borcherding, for going out on some limbs and bringing the book to light.

And many thanks to you, aspiring or experienced songwriter, for picking up this book and taking another step toward your dream. The world's a better place every time someone reaches for sky! Best wishes and good luck!

—Terry Cox

Praise For *You Can Write Song Lyrics!*

Shelly Peiken (Christina Aguilera's "What a Girl Wants," Meredith Brooks's "Bitch," Brandy's "Almost Doesn't Count," etc.)—Terry Cox reminds us that it's not just a craft we need to hone but a spiritual path we need to follow in order to write a song. In her research she has found that hitmakers all seem to have a couple of things in common—trust in inspiration and patience. I forgot how much I had to learn before I started writing songs with my eyes closed and seeing them through to the radio.

Jorgen Elofsson (Britney Spears's "Sometimes," "You Drive Me Crazy," "Girl in My Mirror," Westlife's "If I Let You Go," Boyzone's "Will Be Yours," etc.)—Wow! I've been writing songs for over 20 years—now I finally know what I've been doing. Very inspiring and spiritual, done with love and knowledge. Being a non-native writer of English lyrics, I agree that writing from the heart can help you write things that the mind alone couldn't come up with, especially with language obstacles.

Peter Zizzo (Celine Dion's "Misled," "Only One Road" & "Love is on the Way," Jennifer Lopez's "Promise Me You'll Try," M2M's "Don't Say You Love Me," etc.) —Terry Cox is, first of all, a wonderful lyricist in her own right, with a deep understanding of the craft of song. What she has done here is "open the vault," not only to her own considerable storehouse of knowledge, but to the larger true meanings and disciplines of song creation itself. Terry manages to break it all down to both its spiritual and technical essences, thus making a sometimes amorphous-seeming art form both tangible and manageable. No small feat!

Tina Shafer (Celine Dion's "Love is On the Way," Sheena Easton's "Flower in the Rain," Wendy Moten's "The Way That You Love Me," etc.)—I was up all night with this book! I couldn't put it down—it's that fascinating. Terry has put an incredible "story" together here. It's the story of the processes, pitfalls and payoffs of writing songs. Her detail is amazing, her grasp of song form is impeccable. But it's the readability that ultimately will make this an invaluable tool. She gets her information out in a highly entertaining and accessible style.

TABLE OF CONTENTS

Songwriting—like any other kind of creativity, including life itself—is a collaboration between the miraculous and the mundane. It takes part inspiration, part *per*spiration. Inspiration is usually what starts a song; perspiration is often what finishes it. Inspiration births essence, the spark or heart of an idea; perspiration involves the mechanics of craft—building and assembling ideas into a cohesive form. Inspiration is your lift, and craft is your landing gear. Most writers start with the heart and take off from there.

When I first started writing lyrics, I didn't have a clue about craft. All I had were a bunch of stored-up feelings and thoughts that had erupted into some vague form of poetry, along with some melodies that seemed to go with them. Ironically, I didn't know that I didn't know anything about the craft of songwriting until *after* I was accepted by professionals into a songwriting workshop, based on the quality of my submissions. Evidently my love for writing and a passion to express myself had inspired me to "feel" how to put songs together well enough to get into the workshop. When I realized how little I really knew, I began to lose confidence in myself and my ability to write. It seemed like everybody in the workshop had more experience and was writing better songs than I was. Suddenly I couldn't feel *what* to write because I was so busy thinking about *how* I was supposed to write! I became totally uninspired and even went through a period when I couldn't write at all. Then someone gave me an encouraging analogy.

Imagine a painter trying to paint before he learns how to use brushes or mix colors. He may have lots of fingerpaintings in primary colors or maybe he'll combine whatever is at hand and come up with something original. But sooner or later if he doesn't expand his knowledge of the tools of his craft and the versatility they can provide, he's likely to feel limited and frustrated. No matter how grand an inner vision, it needs vehicles of expression that craft can provide. Songs have sometimes been described as "ear paintings," and like a painter, I had to learn how to use my tools—some of which are the rules of songwriting—to better capture my subject. So that's what I did. Over time the rules became second nature and helped to focus my thoughts and feelings, instead of distracting or constricting me. And feeling comfortable with the basic rules enabled me to know how and when I could break them or make up variations. My inspiration came back—but with a broader palette—giving me more colors, textures and techniques to paint with.

People start out writing songs for many reasons—a compelling need for self-expression, a desire to communicate something to others, a way to have fun and belong to a unique peer group, not to mention an ecstatic love of music, and so on. A couple of writers told me they started writing songs so they could be in a band and get girls. Artist Eric Bazilian of the Hooters, and writer of unusual megahits like Joan Osborne's "One of Us," said he started writing songs so he could sing and play guitar solos. Now he writes because "there is no greater satisfaction in life (aside from Love and Family) than finishing up four minutes of melody and words that express some Greater Truth." John Bettis, who's co-written songs for Michael Jackson, Madonna and a few hundred other artists and was also a writing and performing member of the original Carpenters, says, "Writing came to me so early that it feels like a natural part of me. It's like dreaming; I have always done it. I had no choice. I still do not." Jenny Yates, who has written several songs with Garth Brooks, says, "In a world of uncontrollable circumstances there is one thing I can do—write a song—to say something that might capture a feeling, a moment, an opinion, a person, an exchange, a loss, a love that maybe speaks a truth for and to someone else." Whatever our reasons for starting to write—and however much those reasons and our circumstances might change as we keep at it—at the heart, most of us do it because we love it. And we love it so much that often the best thing about success is that it enables us to keep doing it.

Even if a writer's songs are extremely personal and express deep private truths, he or she usually hopes others will relate to them as well. The chances of that happening are pretty good if your song has three things: (1) it's a genuine expression of something you feel or think, (2) it's in a form that's enjoyable to sing or listen to, and (3) it's memorable. There are no rules about the first point. That's the stuff that comes from inside and has to do with how you experience life. The second and third points you can learn because they have to do with form—how you present what's *inside* on the *outside*. It's sort of like how the clothing you wear expresses what you feel about yourself, who you are or maybe want to be. A song must have form in order to be presented and heard, and that's where the rules and the craft of songwriting come in.

Some of my songwriter friends and I often discuss our sense that writing is essentially about *listening*. We all have feelings, thoughts and ideas that "speak"

2

to us, whether they come from our own inner voices or the voices of other people and their experiences. It's as if the writing part is just a way of capturing what we hear, think and feel by focusing, recording and fine-tuning it with the languages of words and music. Having a good grasp of the mechanics frees you from having to think about *how* to write so you can go with the magic and just *do it*! And when you know your stuff and you're really in tune with your subject matter, sometimes the song will even write itself!

You were dreamin'
on a park bench
'bout a broad highway somewhere
when the music from the carillon
seemed to hurl your heart out there
past the the scientific darkness
past the fireflies that float
to an angel bending down
to wrap you in her warmest coat
And you ask
what am I not doing?
She says
your voice cannot command . . .
in time we will move mountains
and it will come through your hands . . .
So whatever your hands find to do
you must do with all your heart
There are thoughts enough
to blow men's minds
and tear great worlds apart
There's a healing touch to find you
on that broad highway somewhere
to lift you high
as music flyin'
through the angel's hair . . .

Excerpt from "Through Your Hands" by John Hiatt

1 Inspiration— The Magic That Gets You Started

When a mystery is too overpowering, one dare not disobey.
—Antoine de Saint-Exupery, *The Little Prince*

Give way to the stream of life and tumble into the chasm, not knowing . . . it is only when we're lost in our wondering that we can come into the sacred world.
—Priscilla Cogan, *Winona's Web*

Choose pathlessness, as if you knew your way.
—Ursula K. Le Guin, *The Beginning Place*

Inspiration is where it all starts. It enlivens form and gives it heart and reason for being. It's why a song or any other created thing is greater than the sum of its parts. Without it, craft wouldn't be applicable. Inspiration as "in-spiriting" or "in-breathing"—breathing in the spirit of something—is that pinnacle "inner receiving" of essence that seems to enable a song to write itself or a picture to somehow appear on a canvas. It is what writers and other creators dream of, aspire to and sometimes wait for, and it is usually what gives a work impact and longevity because it has qualities that affect and move people on many levels. The effect can be profound or subtle, momentary or life-changing and continue to inspire others—sometimes for centuries.

The Art of Receiving

Like sand or water, inspiration is one of those things that can slip through your fingers the harder you try to hold on to it. However, it is vital to the creativity that is every human being's birthright, and there are ways to conjure it up and prepare yourself to receive it. Fear often keeps people from exploring their creativity. Knowledge, willingness and practice can diminish

4

that fear. Knowledge gives you solid ground, willingness gives you wings and practice makes venturing into the unknown more familiar and therefore less frightening. In my experience, the unknown is where inspiration comes from, and it is craft that enables us to know and give form—for example, words and music—to some of that unknown.

There seem to be as many ways to become inspired as there are people. And each person will experience inspiration in different ways at different moments. It may come to you in solitude or in the company of others. It may come barreling through you as a sudden excitement and sense of connectedness to a truth or purpose—or softly, through silence and stillness, when you are your most natural, non-resistant self. At times you may feel as if you're merely a vehicle simply taking dictation. Inspiration may be triggered by a sudden focus of thoughts or feelings or something someone says or does or something you've read. You may notice that certain kinds of environments, moods, attitudes and people are stimulating and inspiring, while others may be depleting or distracting. The more you write and experience yourself as a writer, the more aware you become about your own writing process and what works or doesn't.

For me, the leavening that activates all the other ingredients in an inspiration "recipe" is love—and I don't necessarily mean the sentimental or romantic kind. How I have come to understand love in the context of writing or creating anything is this: *the willingness to be present to receive a present from the unknown.* This involves listening more than thinking, questioning more than having all the answers and being open to new configurations rather than relying only on what you've already figured out. If you think of your songs as your "babies," love also means respecting and giving space to the forming essence that wants to be born through you to express your *shared* heart in the world.

When I am really open and connected, I feel like a kind of radio receiver, tuned to a certain frequency to receive a particular transmission of words and/or music. The clearer and more out-of-the-way I am, the more amplified the transmission becomes. At the same time, my knowledge, skills and experience act as the filter and facilitator the song uses to find its form. Sometimes I am open enough and the surge of inspiration is strong and mature enough to enable me to write a good first draft of a lyric in twenty to thirty minutes, or an hour or two. What a rush! But sometimes the inspiration plants a seed that has to gestate in the "soil" of my consciousness awhile before it's ready to be born. That may take a day, a week, a year or even a lifetime.

Part of the magic of being focused on writing a particular thing is the "coincidental" support that appears from other people and events. Several times while writing this chapter, I stumbled on newspaper articles or a sentence in a book or magazine that paraphrased what I had just been writing. Or I suddenly felt like turning on the TV and happened into the middle of an interview with a songwriter about writing and inspiration. Two of these were "Puff Daddy" Sean Combs, the rapmeister mogul, and Frank Wildhorn, a theater composer who was being interviewed about his Broadway musical *Jekyll & Hyde*. Worlds apart in the kinds of writing they do, both of these guys exuded the love and excitement of writing songs—a love that never goes away no matter how much early rejection or eventual success— and a desire to share that love with others.

I think for most writers, the more we write, the deeper and more mutually trusting the relationship with our "muse" becomes—even though we have moments and days when nothing seems to come. Below and throughout some of the following chapters are comments from writers about their writing, what magic ingredients compose their own particular "inspiration recipes" and the things that have made writing for each of them a passionate challenge, as well as a privilege.

Billy Steinberg, co-writer of Madonna's "Like a Virgin," Whitney Houston's "So Emotional," the Bangles' "Eternal Flame," Celine Dion's "Falling Into You," etc.

Inspiration is a physical and a mental experience for me. If I really need to write, I can feel a slightly unsettling but exciting tingling . . . it's hard to describe. Perhaps it's a bubbling-up from the unconscious which indicates that certain emotions are in need of surfacing. I learn about my emotional state by reading what I write. Sometimes it seems to pass from my unconscious mind through my pen, almost bypassing my brain.

6

Arnie Roman, co-writer of Celine Dion's "If I Were You," Trisha Yearwood's "There Goes My Baby," "Heart Like a Sad Song,"

Patty Loveless's "To Have You Back Again," Marc Anthony's "Love Is All," etc.

For me, inspiration happens when I open to it, combined with, it seems, when it's ready to come to/through me. It's like going into a trance almost, like opening a channel, taking my conscious mind out of the process and waiting for something to appear. I guess then, that the magic ingredients would be: relaxation, patience, openness, and a lack of conscious-mindedness. I think the conscious mind comes into play once the inspirational idea has manifested to refine the raw material into a finished song.

Annie Roboff, co-writer of Faith Hill's "This Kiss," "I Got My Baby," "If My Heart Had Wings," Trisha Yearwood's "There Goes My Baby," Dixie Chicks's "If I Fall You're Goin' Down With Me," Beth Nielsen Chapman's "Happy Girl," etc.

I just follow whatever feeling is in my stomach—which is really my heart. It's not a very conscious process. Some days I feel like I'm in heaven, and some days I'm exhausted and think that whatever I write is going to be wasted. But every once in a while you find that you do better on a day like that. I just love music so much. I'm a grown-up who walks around with head-phones on no matter where I am. I love the radio—hearing everybody do their great stuff is such an inspiration . . . and fear of being broke helps!

Hugh Prestwood, writer of Trisha Yearwood's "The Song Remembers When," "Shenandoah," Alison Kraus's "Ghost In This House," Randy Travis's "Hard Rock Bottom of Your Heart," Collin Raye's "On the Verge," etc.

My inspiration almost always comes from the music. If I can get something going musically that moves me, my lyric side kicks in and I begin to want to express my emotions verbally. Ideally, I need to feel totally alone with no time constraints. Writing is all about communicating. I have a great desire to communicate with other people, but in real life I am usually dissatisfied with my efforts. So I channel it into my songwriting. There is great,

7

undiluted joy in creating. There is also great solace. When I have been heartbroken, it has healed me. My wife is my magic ingredient. She gives me wonderful positive feedback on what I'm working on. It is a great luxury to have your significant other love what you do.

Louise Hoffsten, BMG Sweden artist and co-writer for "Dance on Your Grave," "Nice Doin' Business," "Let the Best Man Win," Faith Hill's "Bringing Out the Elvis" as well as songs in *Melrose Place* and other TV and film.

Writing is one of my biggest joys in life, an urge to communicate with this world. Creativity is a tool to try to heal the soul—both mine and my audience. I forget my past. I don't worry about the future. All my fears go away and I am so happy! I wish I had the secret recipe for it, but I don't—that's what's so exciting!

Jorgen Elofsson, writer/co-writer of Britney Spears's "Sometimes," "You Drive Me Crazy," "Girl In the Mirror," Boyzone's "Will Be Yours," Meja's "Do the Angels Have a Home," Westlife's "If I Let You Go," etc.

Inspiration is like an energy flow, like jumping on a train not knowing the destination. The writing process is a total now! Magic ingredients: A fired up A&R [artist and repertory] man looking for that song, a great voice, my girlfriend, great chemistry and higher love.

Alex Forbes, artist and co-writer of "Michelangelo," "A Life Well-Lived," "Confidante," as well as Taylor Dane's "Don't Rush Me," Martha Wash's "Leave a Light On," Alisha's "Too Turned On," etc.

Inspiration is always out there, or "in here" actually, just waiting to be tapped, like sap in a maple tree. For me the trick is to actually listen to my heart of hearts—not what I think "they" want to hear—and then dare to say it. When songwriting is inspired, I go into a sort of trance and ride the wave until, a few minutes or hours later, I suddenly snap out of it and behold the result. Time seems to evaporate during these mini-adventures. I think everyone experiences this trance. Some people get it driving race cars, others while cooking a gourmet meal. Personally, I drive very slowly and have nothing in my fridge except frost.

Tanya Leah, co-writer of Susan Ashton's "Stand," Margaret Becker's "Clay and Water," Lila McCann's "I Will Be," etc.

For me, inspiration is mined from life experiences, stories and emotionally charged memories. I just have to open my heart enough to let the feelings flow. It seems to happen when I least expect it, as if the song was there already written in full, just waiting for an opening in the midst of my day-to-day life to present itself when I'm not thinking about it and my mind is on autopilot—or even when I'm sleeping! For me, the magic ingredients for "inspiration stew" are: a good writing book and pen, great collaborators (and friends) and having enough time set aside without distractions.

As you can see from the above comments, the writing process is individual and personal—but there are aspects all writers share. Writing usually involves a kind of receiving, as well as some knowledge of craft so that we know how to use what we receive. And ideally, our art and our lives continually instruct and inspire each other. Things often come when we aren't "officially" looking for them, when the mind is wandering and we're just going about the business of living and experiencing and feeling, with all the miraculous adventures and mundane activities that entails. Whether you're just beginning to explore your own creativity, songwriting and the music business, or you're already an artist or musician who wants to start writing your own lyrics, most writers' experiences suggest the following: Live, love and listen as fully as possible. Pay attention to whatever comes your way in any given moment from the outer and inner worlds that resonates, intrigues and compels you—and use writing as a way of opening, exploring, chronicling and sharing your thoughts and feelings about any and all of it.

Practice Exercises

1. Spend some time with yourself every day for four weeks, around the same time of day and in the same place. In the first week, ask yourself

the same question each day, "What do I love?" Listen for your answer, and as you hear it, speak it aloud and write it down. Notice as the days go on how what you think is true grows and changes and often comes back to something that was always already there.

2. In the second week, change your question to, "What would I do if I could do anything I wanted?" Don't limit or modify your answer according to what you think is possible or what your responsibilities or what the world "out there" will let you do.

3. In the third week, fine-tune each day your lists of the things/people/ places/ideas that you love and have passion for.

4. In the fourth week, take one or two things from your list each day and write a paragraph describing any thoughts or feelings that come into your mind about each.

Recommended Reading

The Courage to Create by Rollo May

The Writing Life by Annie Dillard

2 How Nothing Can Turn Into Something That Sounds Like a Song ♭♭

We . . . struggle with Non-being to force it into Being. We knock upon silence for an answering music.
—Anonymous Chinese poet

Before a universe could be created, empty space had to exist in which it could be made.
—Aryeh Kaplan, *Sefer Yetzirah: The Book of Creation*

Making a thought out of the thought of "non-thought," I sing and dance, following the voice.
—Zen Master Hakuin (ed. Mikio Shinagawa), *Talk to a Stone*

Non-songwriters often ask me, "How do you come up with an idea from nothing?" "How do you make up words and music out of thin air?" I tell them that there's no such thing as "nothing." In my experience, nothing is really something that just hasn't taken form or been expressed yet. A pen poised over a blank page or motionless fingers at a piano or guitar are simply vehicles waiting for heart and mind to drive them into action. A heart is always feeling, a mind always thinking. If you can stay in touch with your feelings and thoughts—and the dreams they conjure—you will always have something to write about. Great songs work an unforgettable magic because they touch so many parts of us. We are moved and sometimes changed by them, and they often accompany and memorialize the most important times in our lives.

Peter Zizzo, co-writer of Celine Dion's "Only One Road," "Misled," "Love Is on the Way," Jennifer Lopez's "Promise Me You'll Try," Cliff Richard's "As Real As I Want to Be," etc.

It's about knowing your best work may come at any time—

11

that you can create something where there was nothing, the unexpected gift of an idea that sets you in motion. It might be a title, a line, a chord change or melody, but it gives you an undeniable feeling of, "Wow, this is it!" For me, the ideas come more readily when I allow my mind to open itself—when I'm not officially working and don't feel the pressure or time constraints of a writing session. Thus, my bathroom is probably the most profitable room in my life—in fact, the lyrics to Celine's "Misled" got written in Jimmy Bralower's bathroom! To sum it up, very often when my ideas are flowing, so is the water—so I'm thinking of having my studio tiled and grouted!

What a Song Is Made Of

A song combines words and melody in a particular time and rhythmic structure to express feelings, thoughts, dreams, intentions or actions of a particular person or persons. The two basic components of a song are **words** and **melody**. According to copyright law, these are the two elements that define and identify a song and protect the composition from being copied or claimed as an original work by anyone else. Ideally, the words sing and give a story to the emotion of the melody, and the melody captures and enhances the meaning and feeling of the words. The words are organized into lyric lines with particular meters and rhyme schemes, which ideally match the rhythms and sounds of the notes and "melodic phrases" that make up the melody.

Meja Beckman, Sony artist and co-writer of "All About the Money," DeDe's "Closer to You," Legacy of Sound's "Happy," Gina G's "Everytime I Fall," Jessica Simpson and Destiny's Child's "Woman in Me," etc.

It's like I'm given a certain word or phrase to begin with. The flow starts, and I do not question myself or ask why this or that word. I just do it. It's the twisting and turning of words that I sometimes feel is not inspirational. Then at times there is no flow at all. I even forget to bring paper and pencils on my travels. So then I know that the period has come for me to collect feelings and experiences to bring home with me and give them time to grow and nurture.

A third element that comes into play during the writing process is the **chord progression,** a **series of chords** (grouping of three or more notes) that harmonizes, accompanies and supports the melody. Music writers either hear the melody first and then find the chords to give it the right emotional color and mood, or they start by playing a chord progression then build the melody on top of it. The arrangement is how the "palette" of the song is further colored and textured by additional instruments, countermelodies, rhythms, voicings, etc. The atmosphere created by the arrangement should, ideally, enhance the impact of the song.

Beth Nielsen Chapman, artist and co-writer/writer of "Happy Girl," "Sand and Water," "Every December Sky," etc., as well as Faith Hill's "This Kiss," Mary Chapin Carpenter's "Almost Home," Willie Nelson's "Nothing I Can Do About It Now," etc.

For me it is often about a sound. The note of the teakettle can get me going to the piano and hitting a chord, and the chord leads to a sound in my voice. I use my voice a lot as kind of an unconscious dowsing—I dowse for vowels. It's a matter of trusting the unknowingness of it, opening the space for some- thing to appear out of nowhere, following the thread of it and trying not to get in its way. It pulls me blindly along this hallway, and if I get lost . . . I just keep following the sound.

What the Music Does

Songs reach us on several levels because we are affected by words and music in different ways. Evan Lamberg, Executive Vice President, Creative, of EMI Music Publishing in New York, says the first thing that hits most people about a song is the melody: "A great melody sticks with the human spirit and the human mind and heart—that's really what the basis of a hit is. A great lyric is important, and can create a standard—but the melody has to be there, or else you're dead in the water." Music usually makes the

13

first impact because it affects feelings without having to go through the analytical part of the brain first. The **major keys** tend to stimulate brighter, happier, simpler, celebratory and more "straightforward" feelings, while the **minor keys** conjure darker, more introspective, deep, complex, yearning feelings. You may suddenly find yourself rocking your head, tapping your foot, dancing around the room and singing at the top of your lungs—or remembering something sad or poignant, crying unexpected tears or being filled with some deep, nameless longing.

Bette Sussman, co-writer of "Somebody Make Me Laugh," recorded by Patti Austin, Hillary and Bob James, David Broza, Eric Mercury's "Sailors," "Include Me Out," Lisa Molina's "Too Much to Ask," etc.

For me, songwriting is about conveying emotion through another language—music.

Great music can make lyrics come alive and take on new meaning and excitement. One of the songs I am impressed with for the way the music adds emotion and depth to an already great lyric is the *Titanic* theme "My Heart Will Go On," written by lyric writer Will Jennings and composer James Horner. I first heard it in 5:00 P.M. bumper-to-bumper traffic, and I was late and annoyed. I turned on the radio and caught the beginning of the song, and about ten seconds into it I burst into tears. I had not seen the movie or heard the song before, but I was instantly moved by the emotion in the music. As the lyrics started sinking in, they conjured up my own memories of a lost love and I boohooed some more. When I finally realized the song was from the *Titanic* movie, the lyrics took on an even *deeper* meaning and I really lost it—as the man in the car next to me gestured sympathetically for me to change lanes in front of him!

Tina Shafer, co-writer of "Love Is on the Way," recorded by Celine Dion and Billy Porter, Sheena Easton's "Love Is on the Way," "Flower in the Rain," Wendy Moten's "The Way That You Love Me," etc.

When the channel is opened inside and you have connected to a true place, the words I would use to describe the feeling I can't say here!! How do I get it? Listening to the music and where it is leading me emotionally—it's always the sounds that bring about the emotion.

People take music personally, and no two people react exactly the same way to the same song. As much as I love lyrics that are all at once intelligent, heart-stirring and soul-epiphanous, I have come to realize that writing great lyrics, at least in the commercial marketplaces, is often less about intellectual cleverness than creating a three-to-four-minute moment that moves emotional mountains in people. The brilliance of "My Heart Will Go On" is in the choice of words that in the context of the music and the *Titanic* film take on a whole other dimension of meaning. The music inundates single words like *near* and *far* with a depth of emotion just as all-consuming as the ocean that threatens to drown the lovers. As the song climbs in intensity (via increasingly dramatic instrumentation as well as modulation of the last chorus), the emotional effect deepens. Try reading the lyric aloud to yourself or to someone else without the music—then play the record, or even just sing it yourself, and *feel* the difference.

My Heart Will Go On (Celine Dion—by James Horner/ Will Jennings)

Every night in my dreams	**Verse 1**
I see you, I feel you,	
That is how I know you go on	
Far across the distance	
And spaces between us	
You have come to show you go on	

Near, far, wherever you are	**Chorus 1**
I believe that the heart does go on	
Once more you open the door	
And you're here in my heart	
And my heart will go on and on	

Love can touch us one time	**Verse 2**
And last for a lifetime	

15

And never let go till we're one
Love was when I loved you
One true time I hold to
In my life we'll always go on

Near, far, wherever you are   **Chorus 2**
I believe that the heart does go on
Once more you open the door
And you're here in my heart
And my heart will go on and on

You're here, there's nothing I fear   **Outchorus**
And I know that my heart will go on
We'll stay forever this way
You are safe in my heart
And my heart will go on and on

What the Words Do

Once the music has grabbed your feelings, an opening is created for the words to start sinking in. The words create song-plot—the who, what, when and where of a song—and thereby give the feeling of the music a specific story for the listener to think about and relate to. The more we hear a song, the more meaning the words can give to the music and the more impactful the song becomes as words and music bond in our memory banks with whatever we happen to be doing or feeling in our lives at that moment. Those feelings and memories are often triggered again whenever we hear that particular song, even years later. Like Robert Gass said in his book *Chanting*, "A song can capture a moment in our lives, preserved forever like an insect in amber." And this is particularly true when the words have named or deepened the emotion of that moment.

In story-type songs, which occur most often in country, folk and some pop, rock and alternative, the words may convey a particular time and place and paint a picture of the character(s), feelings and events with colorful adjectives, adverbs, metaphors and other devices that also help to make the story more specific. In just a few lines of verse, words can establish **when**

16

and **where** the **action** (**what**) is happening, **who** is doing it and **how** he or she **feels** about it. Here are some examples:

Last night under a dark blue sky	**when & where**
We kissed and I felt my heart fly	**who, action/what & feeling**
Tonight I'm standin' here all alone	**when, who & action**
And my heart is heavy as stone	**who & feeling**

* * *

This afternoon on Delaney Street	**when & where**
I saw her and my heart skipped a beat	**who & feeling**
I turned around and told all my friends—	**who & action**
She's gonna be my girl before the day ends	**who & intent to act toward/with whom**

* * *

Tomorrow I will be long gone	**when & what**
There's just no tellin' where	**where**
All I know is I'm gonna get	**who & intention**
Your crazy self out of my hair	**who & where**

It's amazing how much information you get can into four lines. But you don't have a long time to tell your story (most popular songs are 3½ to 4½ minutes long), so you've got to let the listener know what's happening right away in as few words as possible.

Some of the most important words in a song are those that make up the **title**. The title is also referred to as the "**hook**," because the title's job is to hook the listener's attention. The catchier and more interesting the title, the stronger its impact. Although there are plenty of hit songs without great titles, a great title does make people want to hear the song and ultimately helps them to remember it. Many professional writers, particularly those aiming at the commercial marketplace, don't start a song until they've come up with a title they like. Starting with a title helps you focus your writing on a particular idea and use every line in the song to lead up to and support that hook. Sometimes, however, writing a song is a quest in which the title evolves or emerges from an emotional and linguistic journey of discovery. It can be a scarier way to write when you don't know where you're going. But eventually, there it is—the pearl of truth that mercifully appears like a

17

grail from the pilgrimage of verses that have chronicled the journey—the title. What a relief!

In some genres of music, like country, folk, gospel and rap, the lyric is often very important in determining a song's success. Dave Novik, Senior Vice-President of A&R at RCA Records in New York, says that "a lyric is 50 percent of the reason why a song works—often more. A personal statement here, a story song there—but a lyric that is universal and can touch someone's heart or cause their life to change—that's the power of a good lyric, in any genre of music, be it pop, adult, urban or hard rock." Country music loves a good story, and the lyrics weigh in much more heavily than they often do in mainstream pop. Many traditional country songs are based on typical chord progressions, and as important as good melodies are, they may not be breaking new ground so much as giving familiar, solid ground for a unique lyric message. Contemporary country music draws on a wider range of influences and is more and more infiltrated with pop elements, but as Bruce Burch, writer and creative director at EMI Nashville, said, "Lyrics are still king."

What Writers Write Songs About

A song gives you the world of a specific feeling/thought/action in a three- to four-minute or so music-and-lyric nutshell. A song can be about anyone or anything, from any perspective. A good starting place is to write what you feel and want to write about—write from your heart and your own experience, observations and questions about life. Of course, if you're writing a song for someone else to sing on his record, in a film or some other project, it's a good idea to consider what the artist might want to sing about, his style of language and/or what the project requires. However, I think that even if someone else is going to sing your song, the song will have more believability and power if while you're writing it you inhabit the story and emotion of the song as if it were your own.

Steve Dorff, co-writer of Kenny Rogers's "Through the Years," George Strait's "I Cross My Heart" and "Heartland," Barbra Streisand's "Higher Ground," Ronnie Milsap's "Cowboys and Clowns," etc., and composer of music for many feature films, TV movies and TV series.

> *Writing music for me has always been a completely natural state of being. For as long as I can remember, I've literally underscored my entire life as it has progressed. Whatever situation I would experience, from romance to fear to anger, I would find myself translating those emotions into music in my head. Pretty strange kid I was. I guess you'd say that life itself has been my big motivator and inspiration for hearing rhythms and melodies.*

It has been said that there is nothing new under the sun, that all creative works are only re-creations or variations of an Original Creation and that we are only endlessly reinventing the wheel. When you consider, for example, that there are only ten digits (0–9) with which all numbers are represented, only twelve musical tones/notes (A–G, including half steps) from which all others are derived and only twenty-two to thirty or so letters in any of the world's alphabets, it seems we would have run out of original combinations of words and music a long time ago. But we humans love to explore and express and repeat ourselves! In each age and generation, the same core desires, concerns and aspects of life are reexperienced and reexpressed, but in a different context of time, place and people—and somehow that context makes it all seem new. Voilá—the eternal love song.

Love songs have probably been the most popular genre for writers, and collectively we continue to reiterate every angle and aspect of love and feelings of lovelessness that human beings experience. We've got the magic-of-new-love songs, you're-so-right-for-me songs, you-did-me-wrong songs, no-more-heart-in-this-love songs, love-is-going-going-gone songs, looking-for-new-love songs, just-when-I-thought-I'd-never-love-again songs, it's-forever-this-time songs, thank-you-for-being-here-all-this-time songs, and so on. We love to write and sing about and listen to love songs more than any other kind of song. Like many timeless love songs, the lyrics of "My Heart Will Go On" describe a quality of feeling and devotion rather than tell a specific story. The fact that the song emerged from the context of the *Titanic* film implied the story and gave it added dimension, but the words are general enough to tell the story of every heart that ever loved at least once in a way that will never be forgotten.

When you leave the love song genre, the rest of the world of things human beings are concerned about funnels into all kinds of songs about family and friends, life on the farm/street/stage, fun or hard times, being cool or hot or totally uncool or too hot, money, power, community/global politics, warfare, environmental consciousness, dreaming and the meaning of life and death and God. I love the different ways artists have managed to write about any or all of these subjects. One of my favorite secular pop songs speculating about God is the hit "One of Us," written by Eric Bazilian and recorded by Joan Osborne. Another song about God and mankind, Julie Gold's "From a Distance," was a hit for Bette Midler. Other artists and writers who have been concerned with "big questions" in their music are Bob Dylan (and many other sixties singer-poets and groups), U2, Counting Crows, Smashmouth, 10,000 Maniacs, Matchbox 20, the Smithereens, the Police, the Waterboys, Tears for Fears, Bruce Springsteen, George Michael in his later stuff, early Elton John and Bernie Taupin, some of Sheryl Crow and Alanis Morissette, Lauryn Hill, Seal, Blackhawk, and Creed—to name only a very, very few. Then of course you've got the contemporary Christian and gospel markets that have spawned crossover artists like Amy Grant, DC Talk, Michael W. Smith, the late Rich Mullins, and up-and-comers like BMG singer-songwriters Sam Mizell, as well as Ginny Owens, who represented Nashville in the 1999 Lilith Fair.

Then there's "new age" and "world" music, like the various Hildegard von Bingen interpreters, Andrea Bocelli, Yanni, Ky-Mani Marley and scores of others, many of whom have wielded their influence and even acquired a strong presence in the pop and R&B worlds. It's been really refreshing to see Gregorian monks and great operatic tenors like Andrea Bocelli at the top of the worldwide pop charts! Of the many pop artists who incorporate global and cross-cultural elements in their music, one of my longtime favorites is Sting, who often creates a four-minute musical and linguistic opus that combines love and family, existentialism, politics, planetary consciousness, myth and meaning, and maybe the essence of a fictional or real-life character along with a phrase or two from a book he's read. John Lennon and the Beatles, Paul Simon and Peter Gabriel are other long-time striking examples. In "Ray of Light" pop diva Madonna combined fresh rhythmic and musical elements with Vedic influences, Sanskrit chants and lyrics about life and love, memories of her mother and the miracle of her daughter.

Country music has also gained more worldwide appeal. Country songs do some of the best storytelling and life-questioning of any genre of music, in my opinion. You can picture, taste, touch, smell and feel the everyday, real-life scenarios in many country songs. In fact, I don't think there's a single aspect of living and loving that there's not a country song to do or remember it by. I also think some of the best writing in the world comes out of Nashville and the country tradition—particularly when it comes to lyrics. So, if you want to write traditional country songs like Merle Haggard, Hank Williams, Loretta Lynn, George Jones, early Dolly Parton—or hybrid country/pop like the songs recorded by Faith Hill, Shania Twain, Dixie Chicks, Trisha Yearwood, Lorrie Morgan, Vince Gill, George Strait, Wynonna Judd—you've got plenty of great writers to learn from.

What Kinds of Songs Do You Want to Write?

The kind of songs you write may depend in large part on your eventual goals, which you may not know at the start. You might ultimately want to be a singer-songwriter, in which case you'll probably want to write songs that distinguish you stylistically and reflect your personal take on life. This can mean anything from singing your own variation of current popular trends to developing a unique message/vision/sound that may even start a new trend.

Jade.ell, Swedish artist and co-writer of "Gotta Let You Go," "Rivers, Colors and Miles," etc.

Writing is my way of dealing with life. I write songs because they arrive—and I'm able to receive. I think it's important to stay curious and willing to explore. Sometimes I start the day by not saying a word, just resting my hands on the piano to see what will pop up. I call it "the popcorn of the day!" I am trying to live in the moment, being aware of the greatness of that, and breathe in, breathe out. When things are chaotic around me, the songs straighten out the edges and question marks.

If you're not driven to be an artist and would rather write songs for other people to sing, then you're looking at writing directly with artists or their producers and/or writing songs alone or with other writers to shop to artists. If what you love and do best seems to always be whatever is currently popular and you persist and keep perfecting your writing, you may have a

21

good chance of achieving commercial success that will bring you both creative and financial rewards. If what you love and do best is more unusual and "artsy," then you'll probably need to find like-minded artists and writers to work with who want to cut a more original path. It's hard to place unusual artistic songs, however great they may be, by just shopping them around. The types of artists who would record them are usually writing their own songs and aren't often looking for "outside" material—so the trick is to get on the "inside" with them.

George Green, co-writer of John Cougar Mellencamp's "Rain on the Scarecrow," "Human Wheels," "Minutes to Memories," etc., Barbra Streisand's "Higher Ground," Jude Cole's "Speed of Life," etc.

Writing was never something I decided to do; it was what I wanted to do at the exclusion of every other profession. In the beginning, writing verse and short stories was for me both a means of expression and a tool for self-examination. I wrote for years before anyone was the slightest bit interested in what I had to say, but it did not matter, because the writing was important to me. Even today, when I write I never think about someone else reading or responding to the work until after I've finished it. While I am writing, it remains a very personal and exclusive experience. "Write what you know" is the advice most often given young writers at workshops, and I don't know any better way to approach it. I might add this: Write what you imagine, based on what you know.

Stylistically, if you want to get in on some of what's already happening, you've got at least 322 different styles to choose from according to my last count at the www.allmusic.com Web site. Of those, *Billboard,* the music industry magazine that lists radio chart positions of worldwide top-selling songs, covers the following genres: Hot 100 Pop, Adult Contemporary, Adult Top 40, R&B/Hip-Hop, Urban, Rap, Dance/Club Play, Hot Latin, Rock/Mainstream Rock, Modern Rock, Country, Gospel, Contemporary Christian, Classical, Classical Crossover, Jazz, Contemporary Jazz, Reggae, New Age and World Music. It can be overwhelming and repetitive, to say the least. But somehow

22

there's always still room for that next original artist, writer, sound and song.

You don't have to know and decide everything in the beginning. Explore. Write. Listen. Learn. Figure out what you love, and then do it—over and over again. One of the fun things about being a lyric writer is the versatility of writing styles you can be involved in. It's sort of like being a chameleon and inhabiting different personas from one song or project to another. As a lyric writer I've "been" a soul-searching, poetic, philosophical boy; an "attitudy," existentially challenged girl on the edge; and various mainstream pop, country, R&B and rock divas and boy and girl band singers. It can be a lot of fun to experiment with different tones, moods, attitudes and styles of language—as well as to work with all different types of artists, writers and producers.

When you write songs for other people to sing, there may be times and projects when you feel you're "only doing it for the money." If you find yourself earning a living with songs that are not your favorite kinds of writing, I suggest that you still find some time to keep writing what you love—even if you have to squirrel it away until the right artistic opportunity appears. I keep in the back of my mind—and in my lyric notebook—lyrics for what "the voice" said in the film *Field of Dreams*: "Build it, and they will come." Miraculously, sooner or later, in one way or another, they do. In the meantime, like the song said, "When you can't be with the one you love, love the one you're with." This helps to keep you wholehearted, enthusiastic and ready for whatever happens!

Practice Exercises

1. Pick three songs you really like, listen to them, read the lyrics and write down in one sentence what each of them is about.
2. Come up with a new title for each song that summarizes the content and captures the point of the verses (don't worry about matching the music right now).
3. Pick three more songs, listen to the music of each without paying attention to the lyrics. What does the music by itself say to you? Can you imagine the lyrics telling a different story? Like what?

Recommended Reading

The Artist's Way by Julia Cameron

If You Want to Write by Brenda Ueland

3 What Turns Words Into Lyrics

Jasmine comes up where you step. You breathe on dirt and it sails off like a kite. You wash your hands and the water you turn out shines like gold . . . there are hundreds of ways to kneel and kiss the ground.
—Rumi (trans. Coleman Barks), *The Illuminated Rumi*

Many elements compose the talent and skill of turning words into lyrics—an ear and a soul for poetry, a sense of the paradox and poignancy of being human, a passion for the power of language and a knowledge of the mechanics that trigger its potential. All of these work together to help paint a musical, singable and memorable "song picture." Ear, soul and passion are part of your personal, inner domain and are developed by living, feeling and responding to life. A knowledge of mechanics can be acquired through the study and practice of craft.

Rhyme, Rhythm and Repetition

The two most important craft elements that turn words into lyrics are **rhyme** and **rhythm**. Both rely on **repetition** to establish the patterns that make songs musical, singable and memorable. Repeated lyric sounds and rhythms that complement repeated melodic phrases and rhythms help the words feel and sound good rolling off the tongue of the singer and grab the ear of the listener.

Rhyme

Rhyming involves repetition of the sounds of words—primarily at the ends of certain lyric lines and melodic phrases (end-rhyming), and/or sometimes in the middle of lines (internal rhyming). Ideally, the particular places where rhyming occurs in one verse are repeated in another, so that a consistent rhyme scheme is constructed. Since rhyming is about using words that have the same ending vowel sounds, spelling doesn't matter. The last syllable of each rhyming word should sound the same (perfect) or nearly the same (imperfect).

Perfect Rhymes. Words that match in their vowel and also their ending consonant sounds are perfect rhymes. In the case of one-syllable perfect rhymes, usually only the beginning consonant sounds are different: stone/ bone, brush/rush, share/bear, friend/bend, laugh/half. Below are some two- and three-syllable perfect rhymes:

> **stone** / bemoan / overgrown
> **bust** / adjust / undiscussed
> **shine** / design / redefine
> **rain** / explain / Charlemagne
> **friend** / pretend / comprehend
> **laugh** / giraffe / epitaph

Note that the rhyming syllable in each word is also an accented (stressed) syllable, which makes a "strong" rhyme. In a "weak" rhyme, the rhyming syllable is unaccented, as in **sign** and head**line**, or **sea** and victo**ry** (which can sound awkward, but are common and often effective rhymes).

Come up with two- and three-syllable perfect, strong rhymes for the following words:

> fry   / _____   / _____
> ski   / _____   / _____
> stow   / _____   / _____
> twine / _____   / _____
> splat / _____   / _____
> aisle / _____   / _____

Stumped on any of these? Great! This is a good time to consult a rhyming dictionary. Go to a bookstore well stocked in rhyming dictionaries and find one that suits your sense of logic and is quick to use. Sometimes a rhyming dictionary will not only give you interesting rhymes but will also trigger new ideas and angles.

Imperfect Rhymes. Rhymes that match in their vowel sounds but have different ending consonants sounds, or that have slightly different vowel sounds and match in their ending consonant sounds, are imperfect rhymes. Examples are stone/home, gone/wrong, onion/somethin', rain/same, friend/when, love/enough. Some songwriting experts feel that the best rhymes are perfect rhymes, but popular music of all kinds uses imperfect rhymes all the time. Although I lean toward perfect rhymes, I think it's better to use an imperfect rhyme that perfectly captures the meaning than a perfect rhyme that seems contrived.

Come up with three imperfect rhymes for each of the following words. If you consult a rhyming dictionary, look at different rhyme sounds around the same two or three pages, such as "**unch**" and "**unge**."

lunch	/ _____	/ _____
dungeon	/ _____	/ _____
phone	/ _____	/ _____
else	/ _____	/ _____
whistle	/ _____	/ _____
roam	/ _____	/ _____

Another interesting way to rhyme is to pair a two- or three-word phrase with one word, like the following perfect and imperfect rhymes: go there/nowhere, my way/highway, show me/lonely, come to where/underwear, well done/welcome, far cry/barfly.

So now that you know how to rhyme, let's deal with *where* to rhyme.

End-rhyming. End-rhyming occurs at the ends of certain lyric lines and melodic phrases. Let's take a look at the four-line verses below. The lines are numbered so they're easier to refer to, and rhyming lines are coded with the same letters.

1. Last night under this dark blue *sky*	A
2. We kissed and I felt my heart *fly*	A
3. Tonight I'm standin' here all **alone**	B
4. And my heart is heavy as **stone**	B

* * *

1. Tomorrow I will be long **gone**	A
2. There's just no tellin' **where**	B
3. All I know is I'm gonna **get**	C
4. Your crazy self out of my **hair**	B

The first example rhymes every two lines together, and the second example rhymes lines 2 and 4 only. If you rhyme every other line, it might look like this:

1. Tomorrow I will be long *gone*	A
2. There's just no tellin' **where**	B
3. All I know's by the break of ***dawn***	A
4. Your crazy self'll be out of my **hair**	B

Internal Rhyming. In the case of internal rhyming, the rules about placement are not as strict. Internal rhyming can occur anywhere in the middle of a line and correspond to rhymes in the same line or in lines before or after each other. Let's examine these verses again to find some internal rhymes:

1. Last *ni*ght under a **dark** blue sky
2. We kissed and *I* felt my **heart** fly

* * *

1. TomorrOW I will be *long* gone
2. There's just NO **tellin'** where
3. All I KNOW is I'm *gon*na get
4. Your crazy **self** out of my hair

Below is an example of a strong internal rhyme that really catches the ear because of its placement. In addition, the end-rhyme *go there* on line 3 is composed of two words that together rhyme perfectly with the one word internal rhyme *nowhere* on line 4, which occurs without disturbing the regular end-rhyme scheme on lines 2 and 4.

1. They told me 'bout a promised land	A
2. Called the City of Grace	B
3. And I sure would like to **go there**	C
4. But I'm **nowhere** near the place	B

Here are examples of internal rhyming where the vowel sounds are similar and rhyming words occur on the same lines as well as on lines before or after each other:

1. Been on this **road** *all* **alone**	A
2. For 10 *long* years	B

27

3. And the only SPICE in my LIFE	C
4. Has been the *salt* of my own **tears**	B

Rhyme Scheme. Ideally, a rhyme scheme establishes a consistent pattern of rhyming. If lines 2 and 4 of the first verse rhyme, you should also rhyme lines 2 and 4 of the second verse. If you have a catchy, rhythmic internal rhyme on line 3 of the first verse, it's a good idea to have one on line 3 of the second verse. This gives a song enough consistencies to be comfortable to the ear and memorable to the mind. The rhyme schemes I introduced above, AABB, ABCB and ABAB, are very common, basic rhyme patterns. The following lyrics have more complex rhyme schemes in the verses, but notice how simple the chorus rhyme schemes are.

Standing Outside the Fire (Garth Brooks—by Garth Brooks/Jenny Yates)

[Verse 1]

1. We call them **cool**	A
2. Those hearts that have no scars to *show*	B
3. the ones that never do let *go*	B
4. And risk the tables being **turned**	C
5. We call them **fools**	A
6. Who have to dance within the *flame*	D
7. Who chance the sorrow and the *shame*	D
8. that always comes with getting **burned**	C
1. But you got to be tough when consumed by desire	E
2. 'Cause it's not enough just to stand outside the fire	E

[Chorus]

1. Standing outside the **fire**	A
2. Standing outside the **fire**	A
3. Life is not *tried*—it is merely *survived*	B/B
4. if you're standing outside the **fire**	A

Love Is All (Marc Anthony—by Arnie Roman)
[Verse 1]

1. When you hold me like **this**	A
2. So many memories fill my *eyes*	B
3. the first time we **kissed**	A
4. the times we nearly said *goodbye*	B
5. but still here we are	C
6. tested and tried and still *true*	D
7. And stronger than we ever *knew*	D

[Chorus]

1. Love is **all**	A
2. the laughter and the tears that **fall**	A
3. the mundane and the magi**cal**	A
4. love is **all**	A
5. All is *love*	B
6. the careless word, the healing *touch*	B
7. the getting and the giving *up*	B
8. all is *love*	B

Just Enough Rope (Suzy Bogguss—by Michael Lunn/Mike Noble)
[Verse 1]

1. You thought I was dangerous, I thought you were **cool**	A
2. I met you in a parking lot one day after **school**	A
3. We didn't have no money, we didn't have no *sense*	B
4. You jumped in beside me, and then we jumped the *fence*	B
5. We had just enough gas to get to Memphis	C
6. Just the right song playing on the radio	D
7. Just enough highway to push the limit	E
8. We got tangled up with just enough *rope*	D

[Chorus]

1. Oh, just enough **rope**	A
2. Barely hangin' on, barely in con**trol**	A
3. You and me baby and just enough **rope**	A

29

Just to note—the rhyme scheme in the first verse of each of these songs is identical in their second verses, which you'll see if you check out the entire lyrics yourself. The choruses have their own rhyme schemes, which are different from the verses, but they all tend to be much simpler. This makes sense since choruses are usually shorter and simpler and feature repetition of the title. It's amazing how many different types of rhyming patterns writers can come up with, and if you're wondering how to figure out *which* lines to rhyme in order to start a pattern that will become a rhyme scheme, read on!

Constructing the Rhyme Scheme. The rhyme scheme of a song is usually reflective of the structure of the melody. If you're writing lyrics to existing music, the rhyming spots are implied by the music itself—and are usually at the ends of lines/melodic phrases where the melodies are repeating or completing. One common way that melody is constructed, or travels, is to introduce a melodic phrase as a "question" (coinciding with one or two lyric phrases/lines) and resolve it as an "answer" (on a final lyric phrase/line). In a four-line ABAB or ABCB rhyme scheme, the melody will be introduced on the first line (A), maybe answered on the second (B), reintroduced/repeated on the third line (A or C), and answered/resolved on the fourth. The answer lines (2 and 4) will likely be the strong, or primary, places for a rhyme. Lines 1 and 3 may or may not be rhymed; however, if the music has an interesting rhythm on those lines, a rhyme will add to the "hookiness" of them as well. In an ABCCB pattern, the melody might travel like this: introduced on the first line (A), answered on the second (B), repeated/elaborated/changed on the third (C) and fourth (C), then finally resolved on the last (B). Listen to the songs above and notice how the rhyming lines reflect and complement the progression and phrasing of the melodies.

Rhyming helps the ear to hear and remember both melodies and words, so most commercially successful songs have some kind of rhyme scheme. Sometimes, however, the music doesn't seem to need a rhyme because of an unusual shift or unresolution of the melody in a place where you might normally put a rhyme. In more free-form types of music, like jazz and some songs of alternative artists like a Suzanne Vega, the melodies could go on and on without apparent resolution or noticeable spots for rhyming.

Examples of some very successful songs that contain very little rhyming in the verses (except for a few clever internal rhymes) are Sheryl Crow's "All I Want to Do" and "If It Makes You Happy." The choruses, however, are simple, hooky and rhythmic and contain some strong, perfect rhymes (fun/one in "All I Want to Do" and bad/sad in "If It Makes You Happy"), which helps to make the songs memorable. Ditto, more or less, for Alanis Morissette's "Hand in My Pocket," "Head Over Feet" and "Thank U." These artists can get away with breaking a lot of common lyrical rules because they are so good at being uniquely uncommon in the melodic and rhythmic "attitude" of their music and total artistic "package"—and because they are artists writing their own material.

If you're writing the lyrics before the music is written, you can design the rhyme scheme however you want to, as long as you're consistent. If you have an ABCB DDB rhyme scheme in the first verse, try to have that same rhyme scheme in the second verse. Ditto for the chorus—even if some of your words and the rhyming sounds change, the rhymes should occur on the same lines in each chorus. Of course, it's a good idea to construct a rhyme scheme that's likely to reflect a common melodic construction. The point of all this: Consistency that creates a pattern of repetition aids memorability.

Determining the Rhyming Sounds. It's important to match the sounds of words with the sounds of the music. You need to be sensitive to this throughout the whole song, but it is particularly important at the ends of lines where rhymes occur. The only measure of whether or not you've nailed it is how good the lyric feels and sounds, or doesn't, with the music. I learned about this from working with foreign artists and writers who are not native English speakers and are thus initially focused on the sounds of words even more their meaning. Often these artists write the music first, which they give me with a track of nonsense syllables or a "dummy lyric" to present the melody. The helpful thing about this is that their nonsense syllables contain sounds that feel and sound natural to them with their music. So when I write lyrics that contain those same vowel sounds, they have an easier time absorbing and singing the actual lyrics.

This experience really focused my attention on how important it is to match musical tones with actual *a, e, i, o, u* lyric syllables. I'm not sure

31

this can be taught, but it can be sensed and mastered by experience and practice. Some notes and combinations of notes sound and feel better with "a" or "e" sounds, others with "o" or "u" or "i." The more "in tune" you become with what you're writing, the more you can hear and feel compatible sounds. Also note that the higher a note is and the longer it's held, the easier it sings if the lyric syllable ends in a vowel rather than a consonant because the singer's mouth can stay open to hold or play with the note. For example, it's easier to hold or riff on the word *way* (way-ee-ay-ee-ay) than *wait* because the mouth has to eventually close to finish the *t* at the end of *wait*. On the other hand, *waiting* would work fine riffed as "way-ee-ay-ee-ayting."

Rhythm

The rhythm of a lyric line is determined by meter. Meter is determined by the repetition of accented and unaccented syllables in each lyric line, which establishes a consistent pattern. Accented lyric syllables are the stressed or strong syllables that usually fall on, or play off, strong beats in the music. Most pop songs have a 4/4 musical time signature, and the accented/stressed lyric syllables coincide with the strong downbeats, which would be beats 1 and 3. Unaccented lyric syllables usually fall on the weak beats (2 and 4) or serve as pickups to the downbeats. The experts say that this is what makes for good "prosody"—when something sings as it would be spoken, with compatible lyric and melodic stresses. When an unaccented lyric syllable is sung to an accented musical syllable, the result can be awkward because it doesn't sing like it would be spoken—or it could be more interesting and memorable. A one-word example of this is the title of Enrique Iglesias's hit "Bailamos," which would be spoken with an accent on the middle syllable but is sung with the accent on the last syllable. Less interesting, but common, is for three-syllable words like "*vic*tory" to be melodically accented/stressed on the unstressed lyric syllable, as "vic*to*ry," particularly at the end of lines.

A song that's in 4/4 will likely have two stressed lyric syllables per four-beat bar, or one stressed syllable of longer duration per four-beat bar. Thus, a 4/4 song would probably contain two or four stressed syllables in a lyric line, which may or may not fall directly on the downbeats. In a lot of rhythmic pop songs, especially Latin pop, hip-hop and some urban, the strong lyric accents sometimes fall on or play off of the upbeats, which would give the lyric a more syncopated, hooky effect. The singer may also play with the rhythm and phrasing of the words in interesting ways. I love how Lauryn Hill sings the word *reciprocity* as "re [skip 1 beat] ciprocity" in her song "Ex-Factor." Take a look at the meter of a 4/4 verse and chorus of "Love Is All," a Latiny-pop midtempo ballad written by Arnie Roman and recorded by Marc Anthony. The words/syllables stressed by the singer are marked with " ´ "—and if you listen to the song you'll hear that they don't always fall on the downbeat. However, there are four stresses per line, except that on certain lines the fourth stress is "implied" by the music because the lyric line is shorter. Also notice that the chorus comes in early on bar 8, which is a 2/4 bar (two beats instead of four), creating an emotional urgency and intensity, and this motif repeats in the second half of the chorus to keep the intensity going.

Love Is All (Marc Anthony—by Arnie Roman)

    1. When you hóld mé like thís   **Verse**
    2. Só many mémories fíll my eýes
    3. the fírst tíme we kíssed
    4. the tímes we neárly saíd goodbýe
    5. but stíll hére we áre
    6. téstéd and tríed and still trúe
    7. And strónger thán we éver knéw

    1. Love is áll   **Chorus**
    2. the laúghter añd the téars that fáll
    3. the múndane añd the mágicál
    4. love is áll
    5. Áll is lóve
    6. the cáreless wórd, the héaling toúch
    7. the gétting ánd the gíving úp
    8. áll is lóve

When you're writing the lyrics first, don't forget about the importance of meter in giving your eventual song "hookiness." If you vary the line lengths so that your lyric is not totally square or symmetrical (same-meter)—

the same number of syllables and stresses on every line—the music writer will have more room to play with interesting rhythms and melodic phrasings. Just remember, though, that to make the song tight and hooky, you need to make any interesting inconsistencies consistent from verse to verse!

For studying great rhythmic and hooky song constructions in the pop world, check out Britney Spears's ". . . Baby One More Time" and other songs recorded by Spears, 'N Sync, Backstreet Boys, etc. and written by writer-producer Max Martin and some of his co-writers.

Imagery: Painting Pictures With Words

Songs are sometimes referred to as "ear paintings" because words have the particular power to make ideas colorful and paint images and pictures in the listener's head. How the writer makes this happen is by describing and portraying things and situations with figurative (not literal) language. This is where you really get to have fun with writing. By creating different and potentially fresh word combinations to say the same old things in new ways, you express your own sensibilities and uniqueness. Some of the most common figurative, or imagery, devices conjured by writers' imaginations are adjectives and adverbs, simile, metaphor and personification.

Adjectives and Adverbs. These words describe and give qualities to other words, for example, "the *most disturbingly brilliant* eyes," "a *grey soupy* day," "a *purplish pink* sunset," "a *ghostly* night," a "*long-gone* chance" or "a *long ago gone-wrong* love."

Simile. A simile is an expression that compares one thing to another using the word "like" or "as:" "her eyes were *like* stars to a heart dark *as* the sky" or "the sunset gleamed purplish pink *like* a bruise across the sky."

Metaphor. A metaphor uses words to describe something as if it actually *is* something else, for example: "her eyes *are* stars in the dark sky of my heart" or "the wind *is* a howling ghost tonight." Here, the use of the metaphor involves forms of the *be* verb (*am, is* and *are*). Another way of using metaphor is with the preposition *of,* as in "a grey soup *of* a day," "the bruise *of* a purplish pink sunset," "the apple *of* my eye," "a whopper *of* a lie," and so on. The whole point of using metaphor is to invoke a picture of a feeling without describing it literally. For example, here's a metaphorical way to describe a lonely city night among tall buildings and empty streets:

> In the *neon canyons of stone and steel*
> on the *dark splinter of a deserted street*
> the only living thing my bones could feel
> was the *drum of my own heartbeat*

Personification. Personification is used to describe or speak of a thing or place as if it were a person, like some people talk about their cars. For example:

> Old *Bessie*, she had *nerves* of steel
> and *she* never steered me wrong
> *she carried* me through miles of years
> and no road was ever too long—
> I'm gonna miss *her* now that *she's* gone

or

> *Memphis Mama*, I'm comin' home
> Welcome *your favorite son*
> I've walked hell's road
> I've carried my load
> and now my day is done
> Got nothin' left to keep
> the past is a clean sweep
> so *put your arms around me, mama*
> *and rock me to sleep*

Note that in both of the above examples, the language that creates the personification of a woman—nurturing, steadfastness, etc.—can also describe and is *authentic* to the fact that Old Bessie is really a car, and Memphis Mama is a town. In other words, what is being said can be true of both the object and its personification. Using descriptive language that works

35

authentically on both the literal and the metaphorical levels is what makes figurative language powerful.

The term *personification* is also commonly applied to giving a person the qualities of an object or place. However, I think *objectification* might be a more accurate term in these cases. For example, "she's got too many miles on her," metaphorizes/objectifies a woman as a car.

An important thing to remember is to not "mix metaphors"—don't muddy your picture by mixing unrelated concepts or images. For example, in "her eyes were *stars* in the *engine* of my heart," *stars* and *engines* don't have anything to do with each other. However, if you said "her eyes were *spark plugs* in the *engine* of my heart," you'd be painting a picture of the singer as a car (metaphor/objectification), with the woman's eyes as ignitive devices (also objectification) that really get the singer going, so to speak.

Figurative language creates correspondences and associations that are common to all of us, even if the concepts being combined wouldn't be literally associated. Take a look at the lyric of the Garth Brooks song "The River" and notice how thoroughly the writers have used simile, metaphor and personification (or objectification) to convey how important it is for a dreamer to follow his dream.

The River (Garth Brooks—by Victoria Shaw/Garth Brooks)

You know a *dream is like a river*	simile
Ever changin' as it *flows*	extended metaphor
And a *dreamer's just a vessel*	metaphor/objectification
That must follow where it goes	
Trying to learn from what's behind you	
And never knowing what's in store	
Makes each day a constant battle	
Just to *stay between the shores* . . . and	extended metaphor
I will *sail my vessel*	extended metaphor
'Til the *river runs dry*	extended metaphor
Like a bird upon the wind	simile
These *waters are my sky*	metaphor
I'll never *reach my destination*	extended metaphor
If I never try	

36

So I will *sail my vessel*	extended metaphor
'Til the *river runs dry*	extended metaphor
Too many times we stand aside	
And let the *waters slip away*	extended metaphor
'Til what we put off 'til tomorrow	
Has now become today	
so don't you sit upon the *shoreline*	extended metaphor
And say you're satisfied	
Choose to *chance the rapids*	extended metaphor
And dare to *dance the tide* . . . yes	extended metaphor

[Repeat Chorus]

And there's bound to be *rough waters*	extended metaphor
And I know I'll take some falls	
But with the *good Lord as my captain*	simile & extended metaphor
I can make it through them all . . . yes	

[Repeat Chorus]

Yes, I will *sail my vessel*	extended metaphor
'Til the *river runs dry*	extended metaphor
'Til the *river runs dry*	extended metaphor

   The lyric never waivers from the metaphor of the dream as a river, and that the dreamer is the vessel (objectification) that will *sail* on that river " 'til [it] runs dry." And what constantly drives the metaphor home is that it continues to use descriptive language (adjectives, verbs and additional metaphorical nouns) that works authentically on both the literal and the metaphorical levels to talk about the mechanics of how to brave the river. This is called "extending the metaphor." There's also here a kind of extended metaphor that I call "piggybacking" one metaphor on top of another. Notice in the lines "Like a bird upon the wind / These waters are my sky," that *bird* is a new simile for the original simile *vessel*, and *sky* further extends, or piggybacks, on the original metaphor *waters* (synonym for *river*)—sort of a metaphor of a metaphor!

37

Other Devices That Make Words and Ideas Picturesque and Colorful

Alliteration Repeating consonant sounds in fairly close proximity to each
other, like "Peter Piper picked" or "Mary took Mama to the market
today" or "You're my body and bone / my one and only baby/ but
oh you're double the trouble" and so on.

Antonyms Words that are opposites, like *hot* and *cold*, *day* and *night*,
dark and *light*, *black* and *white*, *sooner* or *later*, *now* and *then*, etc.

Apostrophe When an absent, inanimate or dead person, place, thing or
condition is addressed as if it were present and alive, as in "Hello
Heartbreak," "Wake up Memphis, here comes Elvis" and "Time,
don't you wind down my clock."

Assonance Repeating vowel sounds, like "He was *tender* and he was
gentle, and things were differ*ent* th*en*."

Irony Words that express something different or opposite from their literal meaning, like "well, it's another sunny day" when it's actually
raining, or "perfect weather—if you're a mole" (ironic sarcasm).
Irony can also evolve as a coincidence or twist in a plot or outcome of
a situation or story. Another Garth Brooks tune, "Burning Bridges,"
comes to mind to illustrate irony. In this song the guy did his woman
a favor and oiled the same front door that, *ironically*, he'll be walking
out of the next morning to leave her—knowing that he'll suffer the
further irony someday of having burned the bridge that would've
taken him back to her after he's finally learned his lesson.

Paradox Conjured by words or concepts that seem opposite or contradictory
but that complete or depend on each other and create a truth, for example, "She put the *day* in my *night* / and I saw the *dark* in a whole new
light," or "There's *nowhere* I'd rather be / than *anywhere* with you."

Pun A play on words, suggesting more than one meaning, like "Laughin'
All the Way to the Bank," the title of a Michael Peterson song that's
about taking off work to hang out on the bank of a *river*, or the Garth
Brooks song title "Cold Shoulder," which refers to a cold night in December huggin' the shoulder of a snow-piled *road*. A pun can also be
words that sound alike but have different meanings, as in "better give
those words a little *weight* if you expect me to *wait* at the starting gate,"
or a twist on an old cliché, like "*women* in sheeps' clothing" (courtesy
Tina Shafer).

Symbol A person or thing combined with a concept to represent a quality. The color green can symbolize money, jealousy, fertile land or naiveté. Abe Lincoln became a symbol for honesty, and Martin Luther King Jr. a symbol for civil rights. The cross is a symbol for Christ and Christianity, as the Star of David is for Judaism. Money has become a symbol of success. The sky, moon and stars are often symbolic of "wishes and dreams and far-off things." A symbol will often reveal an underlying feeling or point of the story, like "she had $$ in her eyes," implying perhaps that she is greedy, always thinking about money, etc., or, "when he looked at her, he saw $$," implying that he perceived her to be wealthy, or expensive, and wonder if he could afford her, or he saw an opportunity to get some money from or with her and so on. A very rich source of symbolism is our dreams (both waking and sleeping). Some dream experts say that the people we dream about while we're sleeping are not to be taken literally, but as things, feelings or attitudes those people symbolize to us. Carl Jung's *Man and His Symbols* is a good study on symbolism if you want to go deeper.

All this said and defined, it's not particularly important to know the name of a device you may want to use. These devices simply give you more options in your use of language and help make your writing more colorful, picturesque, clever, interesting and memorable. At the same time, any device you use should support the feeling, thought and story you are trying to convey. Don't let your content get lost in a linguistic labyrinth! Your style of language should express and enhance your meaning—not substitute for or distract from it.

Practice Exercises

1. Try your hand at some perfect and imperfect, one-, two- and three-syllable rhymes with the following words:

ice   / _____   _____   _____

ghost / _____   _____   _____

save   / _____   _____   _____

salve   / _____   _____   _____

dealt   / _____   _____   _____

stall   / _____   _____   _____

2. Using the first three lines given below, write a verse composed of a six-line A verse and a two-line pre-chorus with the following rhyme scheme, including two or three internal rhymes:

1.	I had a dog named *Luke*	A
2.	I shoulda' called him *Spook*	A
3.	'Cause he was a big ol' fraidy cat	B
4.	_____	C
5.	_____	C
6.	_____	B
7.	_____	D
8.	_____	D

Recommended Reading

Successful Lyric Writing by Sheila Davis
Writing Better Lyrics by Pat Pattison
You Can Write Poetry by Jeff Mock

4 A Few Words About Music

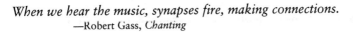

When we hear the music, synapses fire, making connections.
—Robert Gass, *Chanting*

Hear the secrets hidden with the notes.
—Rumi (trans. Coleman Barks), *The Illuminated Rumi*

As a lyric writer, you don't need to know a lot about music to co-write songs. However, you do need to be able to *feel* music. Music sends just as strong a message as do words, but understanding that message ultimately requires different thresholds of hearing than ears and brain. When you put a *t* at the end of *hear*, you name the inner door through which music passes to make its impact upon emotions, memories, body and soul. The ears act as facilitator, and the mind ultimately as translator, of what only the *heart* can comprehend.

When you write lyrics to someone else's music, her greatest hope is that your words will capture the meaning of her music. And when someone else writes music to your lyrics, you're hoping that his music reflects the meaning and attitude of the words. But it takes both your mental and your emotional organs to create a song. As intangible as the ingredients of a good "marriage" of music and lyrics may seem at the heart, the concreteness of certain craft elements help to give that heart a vehicle for expression.

What a Lyric Writer Needs to Know
About the Language of Music

Melodic Constructions. Being familiar with ways melodies are constructed can help you understand how to construct lyrics. Chapter three dealt with this in the sections on rhyme schemes and meter. Chapter five, which deals with common song structures, gives examples of verse and chorus lyric constructions that follow typical melodic constructions. As you become more and more practiced, you will find yourself automatically constructing lyrics in ways melodies are often constructed—even when you don't have a particular melody to write to.

Common Song Types/Tempos. The tempo of a song, which is measured by beats per minute (bpm), is related to both the speed and the feeling of the song. *Ballads* are usually slow to somewhat midtempo (around 65 bpm) and tend to be romantic, reflective, introspective, etc., often appealing to the heart and deep emotions. *Midtempos* (around 90 bpm) often tell a story or describe a feeling with a little more determination or urgency and engage the mind more actively. *Uptempos* (110–130 bpm), as in some dance, rap, pop-rock, bluegrass, etc., will likely have the same persistent motion and emotion/attitude/strong point of view from the beginning to the end of the song. It's very hard to be within hearing distance of an uptempo without keeping time with some part of your body. As writer Peter Zizzo reminded me, however, these definitions are not universally applicable. Many songs with a slow tempo would never be considered ballads—for example, Britney Spears's " . . . Baby One More Time" or Peter Gabriel's "Sledgehammer." And then, a ballad or waltz midtempo like "Iris," by the Goo Goo Dolls, could be counted in such a way that it would be about 180 bpms, which would be super-uptempo!

Music and Studio Terms

It will help you as a lyric writer to know how to communicate in "song language" with your collaborator, who will likely be a songwriter/musician/arranger/producer who may also have a home studio, if not a professional one. You don't have to go to school to get a basic grasp of the lingo; you can learn everything you need to know by hanging out with music writers, musicians or studio techs and asking questions. I knew basic music terminology because I had some exposure to music theory during short stints of learning the bass clarinet and the guitar. My real training, however, was in the studio with other writers. Writer-musicians love to talk about equipment and everything their latest new pieces (or ones they're "jonesing for") can do. In working with them I learned how a studio is set up, the basic equipment most commonly used, and what the progressively more complicated

42

and wizardous keyboards, samplers, computer programs and recording equipment can do. Knowing the language and basic function of the different devices and instruments also enables me to contribute to arrangement ideas or even help find creative solutions to technical limitations.

When you're writing, you or your collaborator(s) will probably be running a work tape. I always take my Sony Walkman (with built-in stereo mike, speaker and speed control) to writing sessions. The recording range and quality are good for a work tape, and the speed control allows playback at slightly different tempos as well. I consider it vital equipment while writing because so often someone will spontaneously come out with something great that we have to listen to again to remember. Or we may decide to go back to an original idea after trying out several options. When the song is complete, we usually make a rough live recording (on that same work tape or a couple of tracks on a bigger recording system) with guitar or keyboard and a vocal melody that may or may not include the lyrics at that point. If and when you decide to do a better recording of a song, you will probably do the demo (demonstration tape) in a multi-track studio.

Now, let's look at some basic music and studio terms you and your collaborator(s) will probably use while you're writing and recording a song together. The following definitions are not classical but are simplified and refer to modern, everyday usage in writing and recording sessions.

A cappella Singing without instrumental accompaniment.

Ad-libs Spontaneous words that enhance the feeling of a song. They are often used to fade out the end rather than have music and vocals stop at the end of a phrase.

Arrangement Refers to the background instrumentation, counter-melodies, rhythms, etc. (may include vocal harmonies) constructed around the melody of a song.

Backgrounds (BGs or BVs) Refers to the background vocals. Some writers/arrangers prefer to record the backgrounds before the lead vocal is recorded so the lead has vocal harmonies to sing against, and others like to record the backgrounds after the lead to give the lead more flexibility.

Bar Common term for a measure of music, each of which contains a particular number of beats as per the time signature. Songs usually contain at least thirty-two bars and often more.

Chord Three or more notes played together that have a spatial and tonal relationship to each other.

Chord structure The sequence or progression of chords that serves as a harmonic "bed" for the melody from the beginning to the end of a song and provides a basic musical accompaniment for performance or recording. It may be written down for musicians as a chord chart.

DAT Two-track (stereo) Digital Audio Tape often used for a final mix of a multi-track recording.

Demo A demonstration tape used to present a song to producers, artists, and record companies. The quality of demos runs anywhere from simple guitar or piano/vocals to a full-blown professional recording.

Downbeat/Upbeat Downbeat usually refers to the first beat of the bar and is commonly referred to in letting a singer or musician know where to start singing or playing—"Come in on the downbeat." (Think of the conductor's baton coming down.) The upbeat refers to the beat leading up to the downbeat (think of a conductor raising his baton before he descends to the downbeat). For example, you might want a guitar player to "play on the upbeats" for an interesting rhythmic effect.

Fade (fade-out) A way of ending a song that slowly decreases the volume of vocals and instruments rather than coming to a complete stop.

Groove (feel) Usually a performance description of playing in front of (on top of) or behind the beat; also used to describe a genre of music ("Latin groove," "R&B groove") or tempo (a "slow" or "midtempo groove.")

Hard disk recording Refers to the recording of musical instruments and vocals directly to a computer hard disk, eliminating the need for tape or external multi-track devices of any kind and providing the ultimate flexibility for data arrangement and editing of parts—including the ability to rearrange vocal parts without the singer(s) being there!

Harmony Two or more notes played or sung together that have a tonal relationship (may be compatible or dissonant). In songwriting this usually refers to the tonal relationship between the melody and the backing chords that give the melody more color and depth. In vocal recording, harmony refers to the tonal melodies supporting or count-

44

ering the lead melody. Two- or three-part harmony is most common and usually is a third, and/or fourth or fifth under and/or above the lead (see *Interval* below).

Instrumental break (break) Refers to a music section that breaks away from the lyric/vocal. A break usually occurs between the second and third choruses, either before or after a vocal bridge (if there is one). It may feature an instrumental solo—a single instrument playing a melodic line, such as a guitar, keyboard, saxophone, mandolin, cello or violin, as well as some vocal riffing.

Interval Spatial distance between two notes, or the root note of a chord and another note of the same chord. For example a third above the note C is E, a fifth is G, a sixth A, a major seventh B).

Key Refers to the notes contained in the particular major or minor scale in which a song is being written/sung/played/recorded. A key may be transposed higher or lower to accommodate the range of the singer or greater ease in playing an instrument.

Lead vocal The featured singer(s) on a demo or record who sings the melody. Sometimes boy or girl groups will have more than one lead singing the melody simultaneously or taking turns. A duet may have two leads, taking turns singing the melody and harmonizing with each other.

Lick/Riffing Vocal or instrumental rhythmic and/or melodic phrasing, like a guitar lick, or vocal ad-libbing or embellishment of a note, word or phrase.

Major/Minor Refers to a bright (major) or dark (minor) feeling, chord and/or key. A basic major chord is constructed with three notes (triad)—the root of the chord, a third and a fifth up from the root. (Looking at a piano keyboard will help here.) There are two whole steps between the root and the third and one and one-half steps between the third and the fifth. So, a C-major chord contains the notes C–E–G, a D-major chord is D–F♯–A and so on. A minor chord is composed of the root, a *minor* third and a fifth—the difference being that the minor third is a half-step down from the major third; there are one and one half steps between the root and the third and two whole steps between the third and the fifth. Therefore, a C-minor (Cm) chord is C–E♭–G, and a D-minor (Dm) chord is D–F–A.

Melody Sequence of single notes that correspond to lyrics that will be sung and/or instrumental solos (guitars, saxophone and keyboards often play melodic lines, phrases or parts).

MIDI (Musical Instrument Digital Interface) Refers to computer language and devices used to connect computers, sequencers, synthesizers, samplers and other electronic musical equipment. An innovation of the 1970s, MIDI was the vital component in developing the optimum potential of multi-track recording. At the same time, computer software writing and tracking programs were developed that could receive and store the MIDI information, which would later be downloaded to a recording device. MIDI provides a relatively inexpensive, space-conserving means to develop arrangements and recordings of songs without a full live band. Most writers with home studios have at least a basic MIDI setup.

Mix, mixdown Usually a stereo (two-track) compilation of a multi-track recording. The final mix is often recorded to a DAT or a mini-disk and copied to a CD. Although not as popular now, some mixing is still done to two-track analog tape because of the "warmer" sound of analog tape as opposed to digital formats.

Modulation A key change in a song (often leading into the last chorus), usually a whole or half-step up, sometimes down.

Multi-track recording Refers to the recording of various instruments and vocal parts on separate tracks. The more tracks available, the greater the arrangement possibilities and the more control you have over each instrument and vocal element of the recording. Multi-track formats include analog tape, digital tape (ADAT, DTRS, etc.) and computer hard disk recording.

Note value Refers to a note's duration, i.e., the number of beats a note is held by an instrument or voice as related to the time signature (in a 4/4 bar, a whole note lasts four beats, a half note two beats, a quarter note one beat, an eighth note one-half beat, a sixteenth note one-fourth beat, etc.).

Pick-up notes Notes preceding a downbeat, usually of very short duration, as an eighth or a sixteenth note. Pick-up notes are very common at the beginning of lyric phrases and usually fall on unstressed sylla-

bles or words, as inconsequential but necessary prepositions (*of, on,* etc.), articles (*the, a, an*) and so on.

Pitch Refers to a particular note of a scale, or to a singer's ability or tendency to sing a note in tune (on pitch) or out of tune (off pitch), which could be either flat—just under—or sharp—just above—the true note.

Pitch control A mechanical device on a keyboard or recording equipment that enables the pitch to be taken up or down for effect or to change the key (which may also change the tempo of the song).

Pocket Refers to a rhythmic element (vocal or instrumental) in a song "landing" exactly where it should in time with the rest of the music, as "it's right in the pocket" or "it's not quite in the pocket."

Range Usually refers to the highest and lowest (top and bottom) note of a melody. Vocally, it comprises the highest to the lowest note a singer is capable of singing. Instrumentally, range refers to the physical capabilities of an instrument (for example, you wouldn't ask a bass player to play a low D because his lowest string is an E, which is one up from D).

Rhythm track Refers to the beat, groove, "feel" of a song and helps establish the tempo and mood. A basic rhythm track usually includes one or more of drums, bass, percussion, keyboard and guitar.

Sustain Holding out a note or phrase of music vocally or instrumentally.

Tempo How fast or slow a song is, measured in beats per minute (bpm).

Time signature Refers to the number of beats per bar and value of the note that gets a beat. For example, 4/4 indicates four beats per bar (top number) with a quarter note (bottom number) getting one beat. While 4/4 is the most common time signature used in pop music, other common time signatures are 3/4 (three beats per bar, quarter note gets one beat) and 6/8 (six beats per bar, eighth note gets one beat).

Transpose To change the key of a song or phrase to a higher or lower one. This is usually done to accommodate the technical abilities of the writer or musicians or the range of the singer. When the music tracks have already been recorded, and it's decided that the vocal would be more powerful in another key, the tracks can be easily and quickly transposed if the music parts are still in the computer rather than already "committed to tape."

Unison Two or more singers or instruments singing or playing the same note or melodic line together, as opposed to singing or playing in harmony.

Voicing The sequence in which the notes in a chord are positioned to achieve a certain harmonic emphasis or to reflect a particular musical style.

Learning to Hear Melodies in Your Head

If you'd like to try writing your own music, take heart in knowing that it's not necessary to be a musician or a trained composer to write music. All the first melodies I "wrote" came right out of the lyrics I was writing. I wasn't trying to write music—I just *heard* the music without thinking about it, and it seemed to come from and go with the words. The task or challenge or gift, however you want to look at it, is about "tuning in" and *receiving*, which means listening without a judgment that inhibits the hearing, or receiving, to echo chapter one. Then you can capture what you hear by simply singing it into a portable tape recorder. Lyric writers often hear "dummy" melodies while writing a lyric (if we're not writing to a set piece of music), and sometimes melodic fragments emerge that are worth developing into a finished melody.

Writing, or hearing, melodies is much more a feeling process for me than writing lyrics. Lyric writing starts out as a feeling process, and I do have to keep connected to the feeling, but soon my intellect gets consciously involved because words are so literal, despite the nuances and metaphors that may color them. Writing music, similar to constructing or painting visual art, seems to be much more immediately dependent on "letting go and letting it flow"—by feeling the music and even momentarily *becoming* it as it emerges.

To Play or Not to Play a Musical Instrument

If you can hear melodies in your head but aren't proficient at playing them with your hands, you may restrict what you're *willing to hear* by what you're *able to play.* My music training didn't go beyond a basic level, and it wasn't until I put the instruments down and started writing words that I started hearing melodies. When I later learned to play basic three-fret guitar as an adult, it was to accompany myself singing those melodies. When I started to record demos of songs for which I had written both melodies and

48

lyrics, I worked with an arranger who took some of my basic chords and gave them more interesting voicings, which in turn gave the songs more sophistication.

The potential drawback to not playing an instrument or having some music education is that you have to rely solely on inspiration, so if you get stuck you can't use technique or acquired knowledge to trigger you into another musical direction or idea. This may not be a problem if you tend to be inspired/connected/tuned in naturally—and, again, you can always choose to work with someone more knowledgeable musically to help develop your ideas.

Practice Exercises

1. Use your favorite instrumental record (without lyrics) to practice coming up with melodies. I suggest classical, New Age or jazz. If a piece already has an instrumental melody, try hearing/singing "counter melodies," meaning melodic phrases that answer or complement the melody that's already there. If there is no melody, listen to the music, let it flow through you, let your mind wander—and when you're moved to, start singing something along with it.

2. If you can play basic guitar or keyboard, get hold of a music "fake" book containing sheet music of popular songs with chord charts. Play the chord progressions of songs you aren't completely familiar with and practice singing your own melodies over them.

Recommended Reading

You Can Write a Song by Amy Appleby

5 The Mechanics— Putting It All Together

%

The master views the parts with compassion, because he understands the whole.
—Lao-tzu (trans. Stephen Mitchell), *Tao Te Ching*

It was as if a veil were being torn from my eyes so I could see the many parts as one.
—Katherine Neville, *The Eight*

You spend so much time painstakingly and lovingly cooking up a delicious dinner of ideas, using all the best ingredients. If you slop it all together it won't be very appetizing—but if you make an art of the presentation, people will want to taste it.
—Beth Nielsen Chapman

A song has less time to make an impact than almost any other art form. Certain song forms are easier to immediately "digest" and help to invoke spontaneous emotional reactions, hooking listeners' interest—and getting them to buy records so they can have the experience all over again! Rules are simply tried-and-true devices for helping to create a first and lasting impression, or what music business people call "commercial" or, better yet, an "undeniable hit." But, as Beth Nielsen Chapman said, "The brilliant songs often are the ones that break the right rules and make that great groundbreaking next big thing a possibility." That's why *nothing* I'm saying in this entire book is true all the time! Once you *know* the rules, you can break, bend or change them, make up your own unique and clever variations and still create a great song—and maybe even a new musical trend.

Song Structure: Repetition and the "Rule of Two"

The most important element in the construction of words and melody into a song is repetition. As discussed in chapter three, the repeating elements in *lyrics* are **sound**, which comprises rhymes, rhyme schemes, alliteration, etc.; **meter**, which determines/reflects rhythm; and **actual words**, such as the title and/or chorus and any other lyric hooks. The repeating elements in *music* are **melodic phrases**, **themes** and **rhythms**, particularly the title and other hook melodies.

A way of understanding the use of repetition in a song is what I call the Rule of Two: *The ear wants to hear something the same way twice before moving on to something different.* Hearing a sound, rhythmic, melodic or lyric motif twice helps to establish it as a familiar theme in the listener's memory. After that, a variation can be more easily grasped and usually helps to increase the excitement of the song. Every element in a song uses the Rule of Two—from the "micro" components of letters, words and lines (sound/rhyming pairs, rhyme schemes and meter) and melodic phrases (repetition of themes and rhythms) to the combining of those components into "macro" sections of repeated verses and choruses (or refrains) that all come together to create the song's structure.

A verse usually starts with at least two identical or similar melodic phrases and then builds into a melodically different third phrase or section (B verse or pre-chorus) before going into the chorus. Sometimes that third section is the chorus itself, which in turn usually establishes a melodic theme at least twice before introducing a third "pay off" melody. One verse-and-chorus unit is then repeated so that you have two verses and two choruses before you "release" to a third different thing—a bridge or some kind of instrumental solo/rhythmic breakdown which usually occurs between the second and third chorus. This third, or "outchorus," as it is commonly called, is likely to be somewhat different, shortened or lengthened. This keeps the forward motion and energy up till the end—or brings it down. In "My Heart Will Go On," for example, the Rule of Two is in play throughout, and the third chorus modulates and contains some new lyrics, which brings more emotional intensity to the end of the song.

As I mentioned earlier, when I first started to learn the craft of songwriting I was very confused about structure—there seemed to be so many different ways to put a song together. Finally, I came to understand that in contemporary music there are basically two forms of song structure: **verse/chorus**, which is the most common, and its cousin **AABA (or AAA)**.

51

The Verse/Chorus Construction

The verse/chorus form has many variations, particularly in the ways verses can be constructed. But whatever the variation, the verses tell the story, and the chorus, which usually contains the song's title and hook, tells the point, the summary, the punch line, etc. Here's how the verse/chorus construction generally flows:

Verse 1: Introduces the story, feeling, idea, etc. Usually composed of four, six, seven, eight or more lines (eight to sixteen or more bars), which may be made up of one or two A sections, or an A and a B section (also called verse and pre-chorus).

Chorus 1: Contains the title and melodic hook of the song. Usually goes up in pitch and energy and often changes rhythm as well. If it does not go up in pitch, it usually features a hooky rhythmic change.

Verse 2: Advances the story/scenario of verse 1 and is a repetition of verse 1 in rhyme scheme, meter and melody. It may sometimes be only half as long if verse 1 is composed of two A sections identical in melody. If verse 1 has a B section or pre-chorus, verse 2 usually repeats the pre-chorus melodically and sometimes lyrically.

Chorus 2: Repeats chorus 1 musically and lyrically, sometimes with a variation at the end before the bridge or instrumental section.

Bridge: Optional. Usually acts as a "release" from the verse and chorus by introducing new lyric, melodic and rhythmic themes. It is often preceded or followed by an instrumental solo. A bridge is sometimes called the "middle eight" (referring to an eight-bar middle section between choruses 2 and 3).

Chorus 3 (Outchorus): Usually starts the same as choruses 1 and 2, but is often shorter, longer or doubled and sometimes includes ad-libs to fade out the end.

To recap, these are the two basic verse/chorus constructions:

I. Verse 1A + 1B *or* 1A twice + pre-chorus
Chorus
Verse 2A + 2B/pre-chorus
Chorus
[Bridge—optional]
Chorus

II. Verse 1A *or* 1A twice
Chorus
Verse 2A *or* 2A twice
Chorus
[Bridge—optional]
Chorus

Note that the A sections of the verses indicate that the same basic melody occurs/repeats in those sections. The B sections, or pre-chorus, represent a different melody that leads into the chorus.

Verse Constructions

As you can see, the basic verse constructions are an A + B format (I) and an A or A + A format (II). There are several common variations of each, according to the number of lyric lines needed to match the melody's construction. Let's look at the verses of the song "Anywhere Is Paradise" (recorded by Stefan Andersson, Jessica Folker, etc.). The original verses are type I construction. I've also altered the verses to illustrate a variation of type I and two examples of type II.

Verse Type I

(original recorded version)

1. Some people got to live on a big city street **Verse 1A**

53

2. So crowded and noisy can't hear their heart beat
3. Some need to stay in their own home town
4. Others kinda' like to keep movin' around

5. But baby I could live near or far   **Verse 1B**
6. Anywhere between here and some shooting star–
7. As long as I'm always where you are.

'Cause anywhere is paradise, etc.   **Chorus 1**

1. Some people want to be where the big money is   **Verse 2A**
2. Some want to be in Hollywood and show biz
3. Some got to be where they know what things mean
4. Others just want to be where they can be seen

5. But baby anywhere for me will do   **Verse 2B**
6. Anywhere between here and that far-off moon—
7. As long as I'm always there with you.

'Cause anywhere is paradise, etc.   **Chorus 2**

(Variation)
1. Some people got to live on a big city street   **Verse 1A**
2. So crowded and noisy can't hear their heart beat
3. Some need to stay in their own home town
4. Others kinda' like to keep movin' around

5. But baby I could live over here, over there   **Verse 2A**
6. I'm ready, I'm willing, I'll go anywhere
7. Maybe we're destined to sail the seas
8. Have-love-will-travel wherever we please

9. And wherever on earth life takes me to   **Pre-chorus 1**
10. I'll be in heaven if I'm there with you.

'Cause anywhere is paradise, etc.   **Chorus 1**

1. Some people want to be where the big money is   **Verse 3A**
2. Some want to be in Hollywood and show biz
3. Some got to be where they know what things mean
4. Others just want to be where they can be seen

(Second A section dropped)

5. But wherever on earth life takes me to   **Pre-chorus 2**
6. I see myself being there with you

'Cause anywhere is paradise, etc.   **Chorus 2**

Verse Type II
(First variation)
1. Some people got to live on a big city street   **Verse 1**
2. So crowded and noisy can't hear their heart beat
3. If I was with you I'd live there too
4. Some need to stay in their own home town
5. Others kinda' like to keep movin' around
6. Me, I would go anywhere with you

'Cause anywhere is paradise, etc.   **Chorus 1**

1. Some people want to be where the big money is   **Verse 2**
2. Some want to be in Hollywood and show biz—
3. If I was with you, well I might too
4. Some got to be where they know what things mean
5. Others just want to be where they can be seen—
6. I only wanna see myself with you

'Cause anywhere is paradise, etc.   **Chorus 2**

Verse Type II
(Second variation)
1. Some people got to live on a big city street   **Verse 1A**
2. So crowded and noisy can't hear their heart beat

55

3. Some need to stay in their own home town
4. Others kinda' like to keep movin' around

5. But baby I could live over here, over there   **Verse 2A/same melody**
6. On Mars or the moon—I'm ready, you say where
7. I'll go wherever you take me to   **(may start a variation on melody**
8. As long as I'm goin' there with you   **or rhythm to lift to chorus)**

'Cause anywhere is paradise, etc.   **Chorus 1**

1. Some people want to be where the big money is   **Verse 3A**
2. Some want to be in Hollywood and show biz
3. But wherever on earth time takes me to
4. I'll be in heaven if I'm there with you

'Cause anywhere is paradise, etc.   **Chorus 2**

As different as the two examples of the type II construction may seem to be, the only real difference is in the number of lyric lines and musical bars the melodic motif in each takes to establish itself. You still have two A melody sections in each version. In the first example, the melodic motif might repeat every three lines, so you'd have two three-line sections, for six lyric lines in each verse. In the second example, the melodic motif of a question-and-answer type melody might repeat every two lines, which would need four lines to make each A verse section and, therefore, two melodically identical four-line sections to compose the entire first verse. This repetition (Rule of Two) allows the second verse (following chorus 1) to be only half as long; thus, you can return to the chorus more quickly, keeping the energy of the song up. Check out the lyrics of the recorded songs later in this chapter that illustrate these two types of verse constructions and note their variations.

Chorus Constructions

The chorus usually features the title, or hook, and should increase the excitement and/or memorability of the song. The chorus is usually a song's pay-off—and pay dirt if it's a hit! In most commercially viable songs, the chorus is the simplified, summarized and intensified *point* of the verses. The energy usually increases by going up in pitch and/or establishing a rhythmic groove that makes the chorus hooky. Molly-Ann Leikin (*How to Write a Hit Song*) suggests that you visualize colors to construct an effective relationship between a verse and a hit chorus: For example, if a verse is lavender, the hue should become bolder and more vibrant as the song travels, until it's full-blown purple at the chorus.

The Title. The most important line in the chorus is usually where the title appears. And the commonly acknowledged place where it'll get the most attention and have the greatest impact is in the first line of the chorus—and then it's usually repeated at least once or twice in another part of the chorus. The second strongest common placement is the last line of the chorus. In this case, the words and melody leading up to the title are likely to be repetitive and hooky, giving the chorus the feel of a double hook ("This Kiss" and "Back at One" are good examples). Except for placement 10, where the title appears in a verse rather than the chorus, the following are common title placements:

1. Title on first, middle (third, fourth or fifth) and maybe last (or next-to-last) lines
2. Title on last line(s) only
3. Title on every line (or almost)
4. Title on every other line (or almost)
5. Title on first line(s) only
6. Title on first and last lines
7. Title on middle and final lines
8. Title on second (and maybe middle or last) line(s)
9. Title in chorus and verse(s)
10. Title in verse only

Below are examples of some common chorus constructions illustrating these ten title placements. Try to listen to some of these songs and notice how the lyric and melodic constructions work together with the Rule of Two to achieve an overall impact and hookiness. Note where the title is and how it works with the melodic hook. If the title is on the first line it usually introduces a melodic phrase that is the hooky question or setup part of the melody. If it's on the second and/or last line, the title probably answers or resolves a melodic phrase. If it's on every line or every other line, the melody is likely to be a repeating refrain or melodic phrase of some kind. Notice also how in some of the choruses the title is supported with words and phrases on other lines. For example, a word or two of the title may be repeated, as in the repeated use of *anywhere* in "Anywhere Is Paradise"; some form, twist or reverse of the title may be used, as in "Love is all / all is love;" or the title's lyric motif may be used on other lines, such as *undo* and *uncry* in "Unbreak My Heart," and the number motif of one to five in "Back at One."

1. Title on first, middle (third, fourth or fifth) and maybe last (or next-to-last) lines

Anywhere Is Paradise (Stefan Andersson, Jessica Folker— by Stefan Andersson/Terry Cox)

1. 'Cause **anywhere is paradise**	Title
2. when you're with the one you love	
3. **Anywhere is** a place that's nice	Partial title
4. when you're with the one you dream of	
5. **Anywhere is paradise**	Title
6. when you're with a love that's true	
7. There's **nowhere** I'd rather be, baby,	Opposite of title word
8. than **anywhere** with you	Partial title

Love Is All (Marc Anthony—by Arnie Roman)

1. **Love is all**	Title
2. the laughter and the tears that fall	
3. the mundane and the magical	
4. **love is all**	Title
5. **all is love**	Reverse title
6. the careless word, the healing touch	
7. the getting and the giving up	
8. **all is love**	Reverse title

(Other examples: Britney Spears's "From the Bottom of My Broken Heart," Brian McKnight's "Lonely," Sting's "A Thousand Years")

2. Title on last line(s) only

This Kiss (Faith Hill—by Robin Lerner/Annie Roboff/ Beth Nielsen Chapman)

1. It's the way you love me
2. It's a feeling like **this**—   **Title word**
3. It's centrifugal motion
4. It's perpetual bliss
5. It's that pivotal moment
6. It's impossible
7. **This Kiss, This Kiss**   **Title**
   (unstoppable)
8. **This Kiss, This Kiss**   **Title**

Back at One (Brian McKnight, Mark Wills—by Brian McKnight)

1. **One**—you're like a dream come true   **Title word**
2. **Two**—just wanna be with you   **Number motif of title**
3. **Three**—girl it's plain to see   **Number motif of title**
4. that you're the only **one** for me
5. **Four**—repeat steps **one** to **three**   **Number motif of title**
6. **Five**—make you fall in love with me   **Number motif of title**
7. If ever I believe our work is done
8. then I start **back at one**   **Title**

(Other examples: Backstreet Boys' "Larger Than Life," Counting Crows' "St. Robinson in His Cadillac Dream," Ricky Martin's "Spanish Eyes")

3. Title on every line (or almost)

True Colors (Cyndi Lauper, Phil Collins—by Tom Kelly/ Billy Steinberg)

1. I see your **true colors** shining through   **Title**

2. I see your **true colors,** that's why I love you   Title
3. Don't be afraid to let them show
4. Your **true colors**   Title
5. Your **true colors** are as beautiful as a rainbow   Title

Hole in My Head (Dixie Chicks—by Buddy Miller/
Jim Lauderdale)
1. **Hole in my head**   Title
2. **Hole in my head**   Title
3. Oh I need a boy like you like a **hole in my head**   Title
4. I need a boy like you like a **hole in my head**   Title
5. Let's just say we will and then don't instead   **This line changes
                                                      in every chorus**

(Other examples: Alanis Morissette's "Thank U," Lauryn Hill's
"When It Hurts So Bad," Creed's "What If" and Sting's "Fill Her
Up")

4. Title on every other line (or almost)

The Secret of Life (Faith Hill—by Gretchen Peters)
1. **The secret of life**   Title
2. is a good cup of coffee
3. **The secret of life**   Title
4. is keep your eye on the ball
5. **The secret of life**   Title
6. is a beautiful woman
7. And Marilyn stares down
8. from the barroom wall

If It Makes You Happy (Sheryl Crow—by Sheryl Crow/
Jeffrey Trott)
1. **If it makes you happy**   Title
2. It can't be that bad
3. **If it makes you happy**   Title
4. Then why the hell are you so sad

(Other examples: Shania Twain's "You're Still the One" and Brian McKnight's "You Could Be the One")

5. Title on first line(s) only

One of Us (Joan Osborne—by Eric Bazilian)
1. What if God was **one of us**   Title
2. Just a slob like **one of us**   Title
3. Just a stranger on the bus
4. Trying to make His way home

Sometimes (Britney Spears—by Jorgen Elofsson)
1. **Sometimes** I run   Title
2. **Sometimes** I hide   Title
3. **Sometimes** I'm scared of you   Title
4. But all I really want is to hold you tight
5. Treat you right
6. Be with you day and night
7. Baby all I need is time

(Other examples: Dixie Chicks' "If I Fall You're Going Down With Me," included later in this chapter, Backstreet Boys' "Quit Playing Games With My Heart")

6. Title on first and last lines

Unbreak My Heart (Toni Braxton—by Diane Warren)
1. **Unbreak my heart**   Title
2. Say you'll love me again
3. **Undo** this hurt you caused   Repeat title motif
4. When you walked out the door
5. And walked out of my life
6. **Un-cry** these tears   Repeat title motif
7. I cried so many nights
8. **Unbreak my heart**   Title

61

Torn (Natalie Imbruglia—by Scott Cutler/Anne Preven/
Phil Thornalley)

1. That's what's going on, nothing's fine I'm **torn**   Title
2. I'm all out of faith, this is how I feel
3. I'm cold and I am shamed lying naked on the floor
4. Illusion never changed into something real
5. I'm wide awake and I can see the perfect sky is **torn** Title
6. You're a little late, I'm already **torn**   Title

(Other examples: Faith Hill's "If My Heart Had Wings," Garth
Brooks's "Unanswered Prayers," Celine Dion's "Treat Her Like a
Lady" and Ricky Martin and Meja's "Private Emotion")

7. Title on middle and final lines

I Don't Want to Miss a Thing (Aerosmith—by Diane Warren)

1. **I don't wanna** close my eyes   Partial title
2. **I don't wanna** fall asleep   Partial title
3. 'Cause I'd **miss** you, baby   Title word
4. And **I don't want to miss a thing**   Title
5. 'Cause even when I dream of you
6. The sweetest dream would never do
7. I'd still **miss** you, baby   Title word
8. And **I don't want to miss a thing**   Title

Sheep's Clothing (Stefan Andersson—by Stefan Andersson/
Terry Cox)

1. At first you hardly notice the pain
2. 'cause they're so good at how to explain
3. Behind a mask of love they hide their loathing
4. Beware of wolves in **sheep's clothing**   Title
5. They'll never give you room to complain
6. The blood of betrayal leaves no stain
7. Behind a mask of love they hide their loathing
8. Beware of wolves in **sheep's clothing**   Title

(Other example: Patty Loveless's "To Have You Back Again")

8. Title on second (and maybe middle or last) line(s) With this construction, the title falls on the "answer" part of the melodic phrase each time it occurs.

Nobody's Supposed to Be Here (Deborah Cox—
by Montell Jordan/Anthony Crawford)

1. How did you get here—		Title word
2. **Nobody's supposed to be here**		Title
3. I've tried that love thing for the last time		
4. My heart says **no, no**		Supports first syllable of title
5. **Nobody's supposed to be here**		Title
6. But you came along and changed my mind		

Goodbye Earl (Dixie Chicks—by Dennis Linde)

1. That **Earl** had to die		Title word
2. **Goodbye Earl**		Title
3. Those black-eyed peas		
4. They tasted all right to me **Earl**		Title word
5. You're feelin' weak		
6. Why don't you lay down		
7. and sleep **Earl**		Title word
8. Ain't it dark		
9. Wrapped up in that tarp **Earl**		Title word

(Other examples: Ricky Martin's "Livin' La Vida Loca," Faith Hill's "That's How Love Moves" and Brian McKnight's "Last Dance")

9. Title in chorus and verse(s)

Let Me Love You One More Time (Michael Peterson—
by Michael Peterson/John Bettis)

So **let me love you one more time**	Title/Last line of every B verse right before chorus
1. **Let me love you one more time**	Title/Chorus
2. Drink your kiss like it was wine	

63

3. 'Cause when I hold your heart like mine

4. We can leave this world behind

Standing Outside the Fire (Garth Brooks—by Garth Brooks/ Jenny Yates)

'Cause it's not enough to just **stand outside the fire** Form of title/ last line of every B

I can't abide **standing outside the fire** Title/last line of bridge

1. **Standing outside the fire** Title/Chorus

2. **Standing outside the fire** Title

3. Life is not tried, it is merely survived

4. If you're **standing outside the fire** Title

(Other examples: Suzy Bogguss's "Just Enough Rope," included later in this chapter, Backstreet Boys' "I Want It That Way" and Lauryn Hill's "Nothing Even Matters")

10. Title in verse only

Last Kiss (Wayne Cochran, Pearl Jam, etc.—by Wayne Cochran)

1. Oh where oh where can my baby be Chorus

2. The Lord took her away from me

3. She's gone to heaven so I got to be good

4. So I can see my baby when I leave this world

I held her close I kissed her our **last kiss** Title/Seventh line of second verse

(Other examples: Alanis Morissette's "Ironic," Sheryl Crow's "Strong Enough" and Madonna's "Sky Fits Heaven")

Bridge Constructions

Bridges are interesting creatures. A bridge is an optional extension of a song's lyric, melodic and rhythmic themes. It gives your ear and mind a break from the two verses and two choruses you've just heard before going back to a third chorus—again the Rule of Two. I've known some publishing and record company people who don't like bridges in songs, and others who don't like songs without them. There are no hard rules about bridges—this is your chance to go wild. But if your song includes a bridge, I suggest that you:

1. keep it short
2. make it sound different melodically and rhythmically than the rest of the song (but still as if it belongs to the song)
3. use some kind of rhyme where the music seems to "want" it

Sometimes the bridge is the hardest part to write, and sometimes it emerges from the song "organically" with your hardly having to think about it. Personally, I love bridges. A bridge is usually floating around in my head as one of the thoughts I have that doesn't quite go with the main theme but is an interesting angle, feeling or "deepening" of the song's story or message. Whatever the bridge is about, it should flow naturally from the sentiment at the end of the chorus before it and back into the beginning of the out-chorus or verse after it. Since it's difficult to study the effects of a bridge outside the context of a song, check out some of the bridges in the examples of whole song constructions in the next section.

Outchorus Constructions

The simplest kind of outchorus is simply a third chorus, identical to choruses 1 and 2. The next simplest is a double chorus—the regular chorus repeated twice. In these cases, in order to keep the song interesting all the way to the end, the singer may ad-lib, varying words, phrasing and melodies somewhat, to keep the energy and excitement up all the way to the end of the song. Sometimes in the outchorus, background singers will sing the regular chorus so the lead singer can riff notes and ad lib with a few words or simple sounds over them. In a third variation of an outchorus, words are changed to add more impact or a twist to the chorus message. Another variation is to shorten it to only a couple of lines and the title. This is sometimes done to take the energy of the song down so it ends softly and quickly.

Now let's look at some examples of whole songs that employ the two common verse/chorus constructions, along with some variations.

I.   Verse 1A + 1B *or* 1A twice + pre-chorus
Chorus
Verse 2A + 2B/pre-chorus
Chorus
[Bridge—optional]
Chorus

    Notice in the following lyric that the title "One of Us" appears twice in the chorus on the first and second lines and is strengthened further by the internal rhymes *God* and *slob*, as well as the end rhyme *on the bus* on the third line. Also note that the second and third choruses are not doubled but extended choruses; the melody of the last line, "Trying to make His way home," is repeated over and over with different lyrics but the same ending rhyme.

One of Us (Joan Osborne—by Eric Bazilian)
1. If God had a name, what would it be   **Verse 1A**
2. And would you call it to His face
3. If you were faced with Him in all His glory
4. What would you ask if you had just one question

5. Yeah, yeah, God is great   **Pre-chorus**
6. Yeah, yeah, God is good
7. Yeah, yeah, yeah, yeah, yeah

1. What if God was **one of us**   **Title/Chorus**
2. Just a slob like **one of us**
3. Just a stranger on the bus
4. Trying to make His way home

1. If God had a face, what would it look like   **Verse 2A**
2. And would you want to see
3. If seeing meant that you would have to believe
4. In things like Heaven and in Jesus and the Saints
5. And all the Prophets and   **Extended line builds suspense**

Yeah, yeah, God is great, etc.   **Repeat pre-chorus**

1. What if God was **one of us**   Title/Chorus
2. Just a slob like **one of us**
3. Just a stranger on the bus
4. Trying to make His way home
5. Tryin' to make His way home   Extended chorus
6. Back up to Heaven all alone
7. Nobody callin' on the phone
8. 'Cept for the Pope maybe in Rome

Yeah, yeah, God is great, etc.   Repeat pre-chorus

[No bridge]

1. What if God was **one of us**   Title/Chorus
2. Just a slob like **one of us**
3. Just a stranger on the bus
4. Trying to make His way home
5. Just tryin' to make His way home   Extended chorus
6. Like a holy rolling stone
7. Back up to Heaven all alone
8. Just tryin' to make His way home
9. Nobody callin' on the phone
10. 'Cept for the Pope maybe in Rome

The following song is another great example of the power and paradox of a well-developed metaphor and play on verbs and other words. By the time you hear the title "Just Enough Rope," all the "just enough" things and situations leading up to it (in both the B verses and the choruses) have made that rope a lot longer, stronger and more powerful than just any old rope could possibly be!

Just Enough Rope (Suzy Bogguss—by Michael Lunn/Mike Noble)
1. You thought I was dangerous, I thought you were cool   Verse 1A
2. I met you in a parking lot one day after school
3. We didn't have no money, we didn't have no sense
4. You jumped in beside me, and then we jumped the fence

5. We had **just enough** gas to get to Memphis   Verse 1B/partial title

6. **Just** the right song playing on the radio   Partial title

7. **Just enough** highway to push the limit   Partial title

8. We got tangled up with **just enough rope**   Title

1. Oh, **just enough rope**   Title/Chorus 1

2. Barely hangin' on, barely in control

3. You and me baby and **just enough rope**   Title

1. I was wild about you, you gave me your heart   Verse 2A

2. We made a solemn promise to never be apart

3. Days turned into months yeah, we were runnin' free

4. You and me together and baby makes three

5. We had **just enough** pride to think we'd make it   Verse 2B/ partial title

6. **Just enough** ride to know the way to go   Partial title

7. **Just enough** time to find a preacher   Partial title

8. We tied the knot with **just enough rope**   Title

Oh, **just enough rope**, etc.   Title /Repeat Chorus 2

1. We could have hung ourselves out to dry   Bridge A

2. But we wrapped it around you and I

3. Then we pulled it tight

4. Here we stand ready to turn another page   Bridge B

5. Some things just get better with age

6. I've been lovin' you since I can't remember when

7. I said it before and I'll say it again

5. We got **just enough** fire to keep it burning   Verse 3B/partial title

6. **Just enough** dream to never give up hope   Partial title

7. **Just enough** love to last forever   Partial title

8. We keep it tied together with **just enough rope**   Title

    (We keep it all together with **just enough rope**)   Title

1. Oh, **just enough rope**   Title/Chorus 3
2. We're still hangin' on, we're still goin' strong
3. **Just enough rope**   Title
4. Oh, **just enough rope**   Title
5. 'Round and around and around we go

In the following song, verses 1A and 1B are both repeated before the chorus comes in. This might be a long wait to hear the chorus—except for the clever placement of the title at the end of each B section. This is a kind of tease that holds your interest till the full-blown chorus comes in with the title on the first line so that you hear it twice. Notice also how the title twists and gathers even more strength at the end with the same words suddenly coming out of a different mouth (*"You* smile at me and *tell me /* let me love you one more time").

Let Me Love You One More Time (Michael Peterson— by Michael Peterson/John Bettis)

1. I've been holdin' you for hours   Verse 1A
2. I wish I had a couple hundred more
3. Maybe then I'd find the words to say what happens
4. When I put my lips to yours

5. I could try and write a legendary love song   Verse 1B
6. But there's never been a rhyme
7. To show you how I'm feeling
8. So **let me love you one more time**   Title

1. It's like a hundred prayin' angels   Verse 2A
2. When you're whisperin' my name
3. The way you reach for me in the darkness
4. Makes me want you like a candle wants the flame

5. As I hold your tender body and   Verse 2B
6. Surrender everything
7. I know I'm never gonna leave you
8. So **let me love you one more time**   Title

69

1. Let me love you one more time   Title/Chorus
2. Drink your kiss like it was wine
3. 'Cause when I hold your heart like mine
4. We can leave this world behind

1. There's the first light of tomorrow   Verse 3A
2. On the wall above the bed
3. Is it real what I remember
4. Or just embers of a dream inside my head?

5. As I'm thinkin' that it didn't really happen   Verse 3B
6. And feelin' it's a crime
7. You smile at me and tell me   (Shift)
8. Let me love you one more time   Title
   Let me love you one more time, etc.   Title/Chorus

In the next example, notice how well the metaphoric title, "If I Fall You're Going Down With Me," is supported by verse lines like "I never felt the earth move . . . until you shook my tree / Nobody runs from the law . . . of love and gravity" and "We're hangin' right on the edge . . . We're hangin' by a thread . . . we can't hold on much longer." Also note how the title is supported in the chorus by reversing the actual title phrase on lines 2 and 4 of the chorus.

If I Fall You're Going Down With Me (Dixie Chicks—
by Matraca Berg/Annie Roboff)
1. Was it the pull of the moon now baby   Verse 1A
2. That led you to my door
3. You say the night's got you acting crazy
4. I think it's something more
5. I never felt the earth move honey   Repeat A melody
6. Until you shook my tree
7. Nobody runs from the law now baby
8. Of love and gravity

9. It pulls you so strong   Pre-chorus 1
10. Baby you gotta hold on

1. If I fall you're going down with me	Title/Chorus 1
2. You're going down with me baby if I fall	Reverse phrasing of title
3. You can't take back every little chill you give me	
4. You're going down with me baby heart and all	Reverse phrasing/ Partial title

1. We're hangin' right on the edge now baby	Verse 2A (half verse)
2. The wind is getting stronger	
3. We're hanging on by a thread now honey	
4. We can't hold on much longer	

5. It's a long way down	Pre-chorus 2
6. but it's too late	

If I fall you're going down with me, etc.	Title/Chorus 2

1. Oooh baby, I couldn't get any higher	Bridge
2. This time I'm willing to dance on the wire	
3. If I fall, If I fall	Partial Title

If I fall you're going down with me, etc.	Title/Chorus 3

The next song, "Love Is on the Way," illustrates a construction that works really well for a big love ballad. The verse melody occurs twice (lines 1–3 and 4–6) in both the first and second A verses (obeying the Rule of Two). Then the two-line pre-chorus changes up the melody and intensifies the emotion, so you're really ready for the melodic, hooky, emotional peak of the chorus when it hits. The chorus features the title on the first line and you also hear the title and supporting melody twice. Notice also how almost every line in the verses and the chorus support the meaning and emotion of the title.

Love Is on the Way (Celine Dion, Billy Porter—by Peter Zizzo/ Tina Shafer/Denise Rich)

1. Wakin' up alone	Verse 1A
2. In a room that still reminds me	
3. My heart has got to learn to forget	

71

4. Starting on my own | Repeat A melody

5. With every breath I'm getting stronger

6. This is not the time for regret

7. 'Cause I don't need to hang onto heartbreak | Pre-chorus 1

8. When there's so much of life left to live

1. **Love is on the way** | Title/Chorus

2. On wings of angels

3. I know it's true

4. I feel it coming through

5. **Love is on the way** | Repeat title

6. Time is turning the pages

7. I don't know when

8. But love will find me again

1. I am not afraid | Verse 2A

2. Of the mystery of tomorrow

3. I have found the faith deep within

4. There's a promise I have made | Repeat A melody

5. There's a dream I'm gonna follow

6. There's another chance to begin

7. And it's coming as sure as the heavens | Pre-chorus 2

8. I can feel it right here in my heart

Love is on the way, etc. | Title/Chorus

1. Oh I know, I know down deep | Bridge

2. down in my heart I know that

Love is on the way, etc. | Title/Chorus

II.   Verse 1A *or* 1A twice
       Chorus
       Verse 2A *or* 2A twice

Chorus
[Bridge—optional]
Chorus

Note in the following lyric that the title appears as the last line of the chorus, and that only the title and the line before it remain the same from chorus to chorus, while the rest of the words change.

Under a Low-Ceilinged Sky (Stefan Andersson—
by Stefan Andersson/Terry Cox)

1. I give to the wind a beautiful thing	Verse 1A
2. Something beautiful I have made	
3. May it go where I cannot	
4. And never tire, never fade	

5. And may the winds of heaven take it far	Repeat A
6. And the clouds not bar the way—	
7. May it take my heart around the earth	
8. And redeem these feet of clay	

1. We are men with brave dreams	Chorus 1
2. Who often fear to try	
3. We are men who face the world	
4. Yet cannot fathom why	
5. And though we say we love the truth	
6. We embrace the well-spoken lie	
7. For we are men who live and men who die	
8. **Under a low-ceilinged sky**	Title

1. I want to learn the meaning of things	Verse 2A
2. I need to know where to begin	
3. I'd like to have my measure of time	
4. Before eternity takes me in	

5. I want to live by things that I believe	Repeat A
6. I believe in love and grace	

73

7. But sometimes heaven is so far away

8. And the earth is a hollow place

1. We are men with hard lives   Chorus 2

2. And many tears we cry

3. We are men who long for sleep

4. Yet have no lullabye

5. We move along paths of madness

6. Only time can justify

7. For we are men who live and men who die

8. **Under a low-ceilinged sky**   Title

1. Sometimes I rise up out of this night   Bridge

2. On better days when the wind is just right

3. Sometimes I think I see the face of God

4. When the moon shines just enough light

1. We are men with bold hearts   Chorus 3

2. Seeking more than meets the eye

3. We are men with folded wings

4. Trying to remember how to fly

5. For we dream the dreams of angels

6. And in our hearts we stand on high

7. Though we are men who live and men who die

8. **Under a low-ceilinged sky**   Title

The potential problem here? Despite how much the artist and I both liked the way the meaning of the chorus grew with the change of words, every time he performed the song live he got the chorus words mixed up.

"The Secret of Life" is an example of a great down-to-earth story song that finds higher meaning right where it is. Here again, the words change in each chorus, but the title is repeated every other line so there aren't quite so many lines to remember.

74

The Secret Of Life (Faith Hill—by Gretchen Peters)

1. Couple of guys sittin' around drinkin'   Verse 1A

2. Down at the Starlight Bar

3. One of 'em says, you know I've been thinkin'

4. Other one says, that won't get you too far

5. He says, this is your life and welcome to it   **Repeat A melody**

6. It's just workin' and drinkin' and dreams

7. Ad on TV says "Just Do It"

8. Hell if I know what that means

1. **The secret of life**   **Chorus 1/Title**

2. Is a good cup of coffee

3. **The secret of life**   **Title**

4. Is keep your eye

5. On the ball

6. **The secret of life**   **Title**

7. Is a beautiful woman

8. And Marilyn stares down

9. From the barroom wall

1. You and me we're just a couple of zeros   **Verse 2A**

2. Just a couple of down-and-outs

3. But movie stars and football heroes

4. What have they got to be unhappy about?

5. So they turn to the bartender, "Sam, what do you   **Repeat A**
   think?   **melody**

6. What's the key that unlocks that door?"

7. Sam don't say nothin' just wipes off the bar

8. And he pours them a couple of more

1. 'Cause **the secret of life**   **Chorus 2/Title**

2. is in Sam's martinis

3. **The secret of life**   **Title**

4. is in Marilyn's eyes

5. **The secret of life**   **Title**

6. is in Monday night football

7. Rolling Stones records and

8. mom's apple pies

1. Sam looks up from his Sunday paper   **Half-verse 3A**
2. Says, boys you're on the wrong track
3. **the secret of life** is there ain't no secret   **Title**
4. And you don't get your money back (hey)

1. **The secret of life**   **Chorus 3/Title**
2. Is gettin' up early
3. **The secret of life**   **Title**
4. Is stayin' up late
5. **The secret of life**   **Title**
6. Is try not to hurry
7. But don't wait, don't wait
8. **The secret of life**   **Title**
9. Is a good cup of coffee
10. **The secret of life**   **Title**
11. Is keep your
12. Eye on the ball
13. **The secret of life**   **Title**
14. Is to find the right woman
15. **The secret of life**   **Title**
16. Is nothin' at all
17. (Oh it's nothin' at all)
18. **The secret of life**   **Title**

1. Couple of guys sittin' around drinkin'   **Half-verse 1A repeat**
2. Down at the Starlight Bar
3. One of 'em says, you know I've been thinkin'
4. Other one says, that won't get you too far
5. That won't get you too far

In the following song, the title is on the last line of the chorus, and the chorus words leading up to it also change in every chorus, although the story should help the listener remember them. If you study this song, notice that the melody makes such a smooth transition from the verse to the chorus that it might arguably be an AABA form rather than a verse/chorus. And in fact, Hugh Prestwood said that "several producers asked if I'd rewrite it to make it more "chorus-y." But this gorgeous, humble tribute to the power of song to revive the heart's memory and emotion ultimately became a hit single for Trisha Yearwood just the way he wrote it.

The Song Remembers When (Trisha Yearwood— by Hugh Prestwood)

1. I was standing at the counter	Verse 1A
2. I was waiting for the change	
3. When I heard that old familiar music start	
4. It was like a lighted match	Repeat A melody
5. had been tossed into my soul	
6. It was like a dam had broken in my heart	

1. After taking every detour	Chorus 1
2. Gettin' lost and losin' track	
3. So that even if I wanted	
4. I could not find my way back	
5. After driving out the memory	
6. Of the way things might have been	
7. After I'd forgotten all about us	
8. **The song remembers when**	Title

1. We were rolling through the Rockies	Verse 2A
2. We were up above the clouds	
3. When a station out of Jackson played that song	
4. And it seemed to fit the moment	Repeat A melody
5. And the moment seemed to freeze	
6. When we turned the music up and sang along	

1. And there was a God in Heaven	Chorus 2
2. And the world made perfect sense	
3. We were young and were in love	
4. And we were easy to convince	
5. We were headed straight for Eden	
6. It was just around the bend	

7. And though I have forgotten all about it

8. **The song remembers when**   **Title**

1. I guess something must have happened   **Bridge**

2. And we must have said goodbye

3. And my heart must have been broken

4. Though I can't recall just why

5. **The song remembers when**   **Title**

1. Well, for all the miles between us   **Verse 3A**

2. And for all the time that's past

3. You would think I haven't gotten very far

4. And I hope my hasty heart   **Repeat A melody**

5. Will forgive me just this once

6. If I stop to wonder how on earth you are

1. But that's just a lot of water   **Chorus 3**

2. Underneath a bridge I burned

3. And there's no use in backtracking

4. Around corners I have turned

5. Still I guess some things we bury

6. Are just bound to rise again

7. Yeah, and even if the whole world has forgotten

8. **The song remembers when**   **Title**

AABA (or AAA) Construction

This form is occasionally used in pop, folk and R&B and more often in country and theater music. The A sections are verses with the title/refrain (repeating phrase) as the beginning or ending lines. The optional B section acts as a release from the melodies, rhythms, etc., of the A section (like the bridge in the verse/chorus form) and usually does not contain the title. Here's how the AA(B)A form generally flows:

    A1 Verse of six to twelve or more lines with repeating title/refrain at the beginning or end.

    A2 Verse the same musically as verse 1, but with different words except for the repeated title/refrain.

(B) Optional "release" from A verses—new melody, rhythm and maybe shorter than verses. The B section also sometimes repeats at the end or before a shortened fourth A verse.

A3 Repeat of verse melody in A1 and A2 with repeating title/refrain; however, this third A may be a shortened, doubled or expanded version of verses A1 and A2, and there may also be an additional A4 section.

Below are three examples of classic AABA constructions with slight variations. In "Eternal Flame" the B section is repeated after the solo, which makes the song an AABBA variation. The refrain is composed of the last three lines of the A section and repeats both musically and lyrically at the end of each A section. If you get a chance to listen to the music, or if you already know the melodies of these songs, notice how the melody builds to the title in each of them. "Eternal Flame" is unique because there are no exactly repeating melody lines within a single verse; however, the melody is very organic and hooky on every line as it builds beautifully to the differently rhythmed title line. The meter of the rhyming syllables falling on strong melodic beats of longer note value—and the internal rhyme ("*burning/ eternal*") on the title lines—all work to strengthen the hookiness of the title.

Eternal Flame (The Bangles—by Billy Steinberg/Tom Kelly/ Susanna Hoffs)

1. Close your eyes, give me your hand, darlin'	Verse A1
2. Do you feel my heart beating?	
3. Do you understand?	
4. Do you feel the same?	Refrain starts
5. Am I only dreaming	
6. Is this burning an **eternal flame**?	Title
1. I believe it's meant to be, darlin'	Verse A2
2. I watch you when you are sleeping	
3. You belong with me	
4. Do you feel the same?	Refrain starts
5. Am I only dreaming	
6. Or is this burning an **eternal flame**?	Title

79

1. Say my name—sun shines through the rain   **Verse B**
2. A whole life so lonely
3. And then you come and ease the pain
4. I don't want to lose this feelin', oh!

(solo)

1. Say my name—sun shines through the rain   **Verse B repeat**
2. A whole life so lonely
3. And then you come and ease the pain
4. I don't want to lose this feelin', oh

1. Close your eyes, give me your hand   **Verse A3**
2. Do you feel my heart beating?
3. Do you understand?
4. Do you feel the same?   **Refrain starts**
5. Am I only dreaming
6. Or is this burning an **eternal flame?**   **Title**

Typical of a lot of blues tunes, this next song has a lot of repeating melodies, and the transition to the title refrain is very subtle.

Belly-Up Blues (Louise Hoffsten—by Louise Hoffsten/Terry Cox)
1. He drank all my sweet love   **Verse A1**
2. Emptied my cup
3. Picked this poor heart clean
4. Till it went **belly-up**
5. Talkin' 'bout nothin' left to lose
6. It's an old story, but've you heard the news?
7. I've gone **belly-up blues**   **Title**

1. What he gave with one hand   **Verse A2**
2. The other took back
3. Rode on my freight train
4. Then drove it off the track
5. Talkin' 'bout nothin' he didn't use

6. I can't walk one mile more in these hurtin' shoes
7. Talkin' **belly-up blues**　　　　　　　　　　Title

1. I am fed up　　　　　　　　　　Verse B
2. with these low-down days
3. I pray to heaven
4. for some hell to raise—

1. But ain't nothin' hot around　　　　　　　　　　Verse A3
2. Pickins' are slim
3. All my love went out
4. And none is comin' in
5. Talkin' 'bout nothin' from which to choose
6. No kind of offer I could even refuse
7. Talkin' **belly-up, belly-up blues**　　　　　　　　　　Title
8. Love is a mystery, and I'm all out of clues
9. Talkin' **belly-up, belly-up blues**　　　　　　　　　　Title

What I love about this next AABA lyric, Beth Nielsen Chapman's "Every December Sky," is how the *form* of the lyric mirrors its *meaning* so beautifully. The title comes full circle—beginning the first sentence of the lyric and ending the last—while the ending ("every December sky") contains the potential ("spring-filled trees") for yet another beginning.

Every December Sky (written and recorded by Beth Nielsen Chapman)
1. **Every December sky**　　　　　　　　　　Verse 1A/Title
2. Must lose its faith in leaves
3. And dream of the spring inside the trees
4. How heavy the empty heart
5. How light the heart that's full
6. Sometimes I have to trust what I can't know
7. Sometimes I have to trust what I can't know

1. We're walking to paradise   **Verse 2A**
2. The angels lend us shoes
3. 'Cause all that we own we'll come to lose
4. And heaven is not so far
5. Outside this womb of words
6. With every rose that blooms my soul is assured
7. Just like a song I've known, yet still unheard

1. Every leaf of fire lets go   **Verse B**
2. Melting in the arms of earth and snow

1. If I could hold you now   **Verse 3A (partial)**
2. You'd enter like a sigh
3. You'd be the wind that blows the answer to why
4. You'd be the spring-filled trees
5. Of **every December sky**   **Title**

Most of these constructions have become second nature to me over the years, which happens with all experienced writers eventually. I have to admit, however, that writing this book and studying these song examples myself have strengthened my own writing—sort of like I've had a "software" update. There's a lot of potential power in downloading new information and letting it all slide back into your subconscious "database" to give your inspired ideas more choices to access during the formation process. This helps to bring closer together the worlds of inspiration and mechanics—the "heaven and earth" of creativity. I agree with Beth Chapman when she says that "inspiration, the first breath of something and the creative place it comes from, has its own ideas about organization." An idea often seems to come with its own start-up kit to make sure it has a leg to stand on—but then it relies on your expertise to help it go the distance!

Practice Exercises

1. Analyze the rhyme schemes of all the songs in this chapter, noticing how the rhymes support melodic constructions.
2. Pick five other songs you like and analyze all the components: verses, choruses, bridge, where the title occurs, rhyme schemes. Make a note

of each place where the Rule of Two is in play.

3. Study a CD of your favorite artist who writes his or her own songs, and do the same analysis as in #2. Are there stylistic consistencies from one song to another? If so, what?

Recommended Reading

The Craft of Lyric Writing by Sheila Davis

How to Write a Hit Song by Molly-Ann Leiken

6 Collaboration—When Two or More Are Gathered in Creativity's Name

Wherever two or more are gathered, there shall I be.
—The Holy Bible

A tunnel would be possible, a bridge would also do,
But wouldn't it be better to amalgamate the two?
—Piet Hein, *Grooks*

One eye can see, but it takes both to give perspective.
—Stephen and Ondrea Levine, *Embracing the Beloved*

Collaboration is a very special experience. A good day is creativity multiplied by however many people are in the room, each one sparking and fueling the other's ideas, till a great song is born that no one would've written alone or with any other combination of people. A not-so-good day is two or more people sitting in a room feeling stymied and stagnant—like trying to swim in a river that's all rocks and no flow. But not to discourage. One of the saving graces of collaboration is that when all else fails, the fear of failure in the presence of another will likely inspire you to come up with *something*—even something great!

I have never been in a writing session where I didn't contribute substantially, but "scrappy dog thoughts" sometimes still trample through my mind beforehand (especially in a new collaboration) like, "I wonder if *this* is the time I won't be able to come up with anything? Will I be able to think, to be inspired in the same room with this person? What will they think of what I do come up with, or if I don't? Will I be too poetic for them, or too banal?" But creativity, like love, has a heart, mind and momentum of its own—and when it's combined and shared it usually multiplies itself. And, thankfully, when a song wants to come through, often it just barrels right past your fears.

Beth Nielsen Chapman, artist-writer who writes music and lyrics and collaborates with Annie Roboff, Eric Kaz, Joe Henry, Mary Chapin Carpenter, Bill Lloyd, Gary Nicholson, etc.

When I'm writing by myself, I'm going into the unknown by myself. What I like about collaboration is that it's also fun to go into someone else's unknown and get inside their life and find the common denominators. I really am drawn to writing with people who have a strength that I want to strengthen up in myself—and I really do learn if I'm half paying attention. If I'm not, it's time to go to lunch. What I also love about writing with someone is learning and relearning and re-underlining for myself that . . . the best stuff is always so conversational, that if you took it out of a song you could stick it on a street corner in New York and two people would be having it come out of their mouths.

Who Does What First?

No two collaborations are alike, and there are as many ways to write a song as there are people coming together to do it. However the collective creative dynamics play out, there are basically three ways that I, as a lyric writer, have worked: (1) the music writer gives me the music, and I write the lyric to the melody; (2) I give the music writer a whole or partial lyric (probably one verse and chorus), and she writes music to it (and sometimes I contribute); or (3) we sit in a room together and come up with something from scratch. If you're writing with another writer, you usually try to accommodate each other's ways of working, so long as you can each still contribute your best work. If you're working with an artist or act that plans to contribute significantly to the writing, you may be asked to write in a way that works best for them—or you'll at least need to be open to whatever comes! And this is where it comes in handy to be versatile in your working styles.

Billy Steinberg, usually the lyric writer in his collaborations, also a music writer and has worked extensively with Tom Kelly, Rick Nowels, Marie Claire D'Ubaldo, Chrissie Hynde, etc.

85

> *I am a better lyricist than musician. I always write the lyrics before the music. For me, words inspire music. I wrote my first hit alone—"How Do I Make You" by Linda Rondstadt. In a collaborator, I look for someone who excels at what I lack. In collaborating with a writer, the goal is to write a song that will appeal to an artist. Tom Kelly and I wrote "Like a Virgin" before we had ever heard of Madonna. Most A&R people laughed at us and doubted that anyone would sing a song called "Like a Virgin." It worked perfectly for Madonna but wouldn't have worked as well for any other artist. In contrast, our song "True Colors" (Cyndi Lauper, Phil Collins, etc.) has a more universal appeal and could have been recorded by many different artists.*

The good thing about writing with an artist is that you don't have to go looking for somebody to record the song after you've written it, unless for some reason the artist decides not to do it. Hopefully, together you can write the song till the artist loves it and sounds great singing it, which saves all the wondering and speculation that occurs when you're writing for a *type* of artist rather than a specific artist.

> *George Green,* lyricist, collaborator with John Cougar Mellencamp, Steve Dorff, Jude Cole, Daryl Hall, Kent Agee, etc.
> *Because I am a lyricist, all of my songwriting is collaboration. I rarely, however, write in the same room with someone else. This is just what works for me. Nearly every song I've written, I wrote the lyrics before my collaborator wrote the melody. I find I write better this way, and my collaborators have told me that they do, too. Writing with an artist is of course preferable for me, because it skips the step of trying to find a home for a song.*

Working with an artist can be an experience that goes way beyond writing. You've got to *feel* where the artist is and figure out how to translate that into a song that communicates her particular artistic vision (and also ultimately satisfies the producer and record company). If you're working on a whole record with an artist, you may wind up spending a lot of time together. That time—and possibly friendship—can yield a lot of information, energy and emotion, which gets translated into the actual writing. I've worked with a couple of different artists on whole record projects. On one project, the artist and I holed up on an island off the coast of Sweden and wrote nearly twenty songs in three weeks. With another I co-wrote fifteen songs or so over the course of one and one-half eventful and intense years in her life. In each situation, I tried to align myself with the artist's mental and emotional state. Part of the passion and enthusiasm I brought to the picture was an ability to relate from my own life, as well as share my collaborator's artistic vision. Songwriter Shelly Peiken, who worked with Meredith Brooks on the album that yielded the hit single "Bitch," seems to have had a similar experience in terms of the songs emerging out of the mix of life and music.

Shelly Peiken, co-writer of Brandy's "Almost Doesn't Count," Meredith Brooks's "Bitch," Christina Aguilera's "What a Girl Wants," The Pretenders' "Human," and collaborates with Meredith Brooks, Guy Roche, Howie Dorough (Backstreet Boys), Albert Hammond, Geoffrey Williams, etc.

"Bitch" was written on an acoustic guitar in a little room in my house. No drum machine, no amps. Not to sound too cosmic, but I felt like Meredith and I just channeled that one together. We shared a common ground when it came to the subject matter—we were really in sync. Meredith played the guitar, although I had some chord change ideas. She had a line, I had a line, and so on. We told the story. It happened quickly (except for the last line in the chorus, which took another two days). When she left my house that day we knew we had done something special. As far as the other songs on the record, we took a lot of hikes together, and most of the songs came from what we talked about on them. It helps when you spend time with an artist you're working with that intensely. Taking material from real life makes you feel like you're writing about something true, not just making stuff up. And the truth is always more interesting.

87

An artist who is an inexperienced writer can learn a lot by working with established, experienced writers. Dave Novik of RCA says, "Collaboration is the best way for an artist to learn the skills required to write great songs. If they are signed because of their vocal or performance ability, often they require outside material. Eventually, they will want to write themselves and will have learned a lot by watching the writers employed on their project create songs on their behalf." If you find yourself in a writing session with an artist who is an inexperienced writer, don't think that there's not something there for you to learn, too. Sometimes new writers are vague about their vision, and your challenge is to be focused and help them to focus. Sometimes they are very clear, and it's your job to really *hear* what they're saying and write it in words that capture exactly what they mean. An artist's vocal ability or unique style can stimulate your writing into some new and interesting areas. In addition, if a new artist is involved, you may have the opportunity to produce, if you're so inclined.

Finding the Right Partner(s) in Rhyme

I used to write music and lyrics both, but at a certain point I decided to focus on what I did best and could be the most versatile at, which was writing lyrics. That meant I would always be working with one or more collaborators, so naturally, finding great melody writers to work with became very important for me. If you write great lyrics but the music isn't happening, the song will likely never get cut. On the other hand, if the music is great, even if there's some question about the lyrics, the song still has a good chance at getting cut— particularly in pop music. Artists and businesspeople often feel that words can be changed more readily to accommodate hit music.

John Bettis, lyricist who has worked with the likes of Richard Carpenter, Walter Afanasieff, Steve Dorff, Burt Bachrach, Michael Peterson, etc.

A collaborator is always a gift. When they are brilliant they are a miracle that you get to be a part of. No two are the same. Find one that makes you more than you thought you could be and hang on like grim death. I have sailed wide waters with good companions more often than I deserve. Writing alone is overrated. We have had great ones. Cole Porter. Bob Dylan. Paul Simon. Hank Williams. Prince and others. Cobain comes to mind. However, if you look through a catalog of standards, you really want to be half of Lennon/McCartney, Jagger/ Richards, Rogers/Hart, Bachrach/David, Harris/Lewis. More value. More variation. Deeper roots. One and one make way more than two, usually.

Summarizing the experience of my writer friends as well as my own, below are seven pointers for finding the right collaborator for you and the song or project you're working on.

1. *Be the best* you *can be at what you do and always be ready to try something new.*

You should be able to hold up your end and to be a sounding board for what your partner does as well. Some of this will come naturally in the evolution of your own expertise. Know your strengths and regard your "weaknesses" as areas of challenge. I prefer the word *challenge* because writers are always growing, and you never know what magic you might be able to do with the right mix of collaborators and ideas. When I decided to stop writing music on my own and focus on writing lyrics, I grew into thinking that I *couldn't* write melodies. I didn't need to, anyway, if I was working with great melody writers. However, once in a while I work with somebody who isn't having a good day, and somehow I wind up writing a lot of the melody as well as the lyric. And wouldn't you know, a couple of times the song got cut.

Annie Roboff, music writer, occasional lyricsist, collaborator with Matraca Berg, Beth Nielsen Chapman, Mary Chapin Carpenter, Arnie Roman, Bob DiPiero, Marcus Hummon, etc.

I like to write from the music first. It's very important to surround yourself with people who are excellent so that when they have an opinion, you actually will follow it. It's important to trust your instincts if you don't think a line is right. For example, I might really be intimidated to say to a Beth Chapman, "I don't think this line is good enough," but even if you think somebody knows better than you, you have to say your truth because it usually leads to something better. It's important not

89

to be invested in being right or wrong, but to really let an idea float. Instead of saying "you're wrong," you live with it and see—but then again, if you feel really strongly, you fight for it. Know who you're writing with and respect their strengths, and let them feel comfortable to express themselves. I don't do the same things with Arnie [Roman] that I do with Beth [Chapman] or Matraca [Berg] or Bob [DiPiero].

2. Find others who are good at what they do and complement, stimulate and complete what you do.

If you're primarily a lyric writer, you need a music writer who's at least at your level of development. Understand that seasoned, successful writers rarely want to work with a beginning writer unless the beginner is brilliant, has a brilliant idea for a song, is connected to a brilliant opportunity for getting a song placed or is an artist with a record deal or good chance for one. The more experienced a writer you become, the more experienced your collaborators will be—again, that's the natural evolution of expertise. The artist exception can be very good for artists and writers both. Many new artists' careers have been made via hit songs written by or with a well-known, great writer, and many writers' careers have taken off by working on new artist projects that wound up becoming worldwide hits.

Eric Bazilian, artist-writer of music and lyrics, collaborator on several records with Rob Hyman for their band The Hooters and other projects, and collaborator with Joan Osborne, Rick Chertoff, Cyndi Lauper, Amanda Marshall, Des'ree, etc.

Collaboration is fun if there's a good personal vibe happening. I can't work otherwise. I need to love the one I'm with in one way or another or it's all business, and I can't work that way. I rely on my collaborator for willingness to go where I go and take me someplace interesting and not to try and sell me on some cheesy cliché because it's worked before for them or someone else. [When writing alone], I'm my own harshest critic and biggest fan. I get to take the long roller-coaster ride without anyone else telling me how good it is when in my heart I know [it's not], or discouraging me when I know there's a real gem in there which hasn't yet made its presence known in a way that Mortals can understand.

Also note that in today's pop music world, a lyric writer's possibility of success increases if the music writer(s) not only can write a great melody but also can arrange and produce a record-quality track that sounds current and fresh—or have arrangers and studio people who can. In New York and Los Angeles, writers often work on machines (samplers, synthesizers, etc.) that simulate and record guitars and keyboards, and often it's the writer-producer playing everything. In the pop and R&B world, the backing track is often vital to the effect and salability of a song; therefore, a track writer who hasn't contributed to melody or lyrics is still considered an important member of a collaboration team and often shares in the writing splits of the song. Nashville and the world of country music is a whole other thing. A song usually gets written by two (or more) people in a room playing guitar or keyboard, who then take it into a studio with hired live musicians who play together until it feels right and the song is recorded. And once in a while, a writer still sits down with a guitar in a record or publishing company office, or in an artist's living room or kitchen, and plays the song live.

Peter Zizzo, writer of music and/or lyrics, collaborator with Arnie Roman, Michael McDonald, John Bettis, Celine Dion, Andy Marvel, Tina Shafer, Jimmy Bralower, etc.

I love writing solo. It's the purest way to write, by far, but the hardest way to write commercially. I've had good success in this area and plan to do it more and more. The two biggest challenges I find in writing alone are having no one to bounce anything off and keeping appointments with myself. I love collaborations. I can wear either the lyricist or the music guy hat. I have no preference. Someone else's originality almost always brings out your own. That's why I prefer not trying to jump on trend bandwagons. It will sap the creative energy of the writers if they're looking over their shoulders the whole time, listening to other people's records and weighing themselves down. Start from nowhere together, or from one person's burst of some-

thing, and let it go where it goes. Every writer in the room has valid, timeless influences that will infuse the work, whether they're aware of it or not!

---

3. Find someone who writes well in the genres or styles of music you want to do.

Unlike lyric writers, who can often write well in a wide variety of styles and attitudes, most music writers have two or three or so styles that they're strong in and others they love to explore occasionally. For example, some write great ballads but have a harder time with uptempos. Some are great at pop songs but don't have the innate "soul" for R&B. Some are less strong with melodies but are great arrangers, track writers and/or editors of melody and lyric. We can't write authentically in every genre and medium. It's usually easier for me as a lyric writer to inhabit and move between the language styles and vocabularies of pop, rock, R&B, country, jazz, etc., than for the music writer, who also has to be concerned with sound, harmony and production. But, of course, I have to draw the line, too, on what I feel I can do. For me, that line is urban, hip-hop, rap, etc. I wouldn't be an authentic creator in those languages. I don't live and breathe there, and there's no way I could top the inspired brilliance and authenticity of some of those who do. But again, never say never—when there's a magic and momentum between writers, together they may go way beyond their usual artistic arenas and individual limitations.

4. Be respectful to your collaborator's opinions and ideas, and be willing to rewrite.

We all love the experience of having something come out perfect in the first writing. Whether you're a beginning or a seasoned writer, your enthusiasm and passion can help to inspire mini-epiphanies of songs that just seem to rush out of you. Often the difference with the experienced writer, however, is the willingness to go back and take another look with a more objective eye—which may be your collaborator's. I have found again and again that when there's something I'm not quite settled or satisfied with in a lyric I've written, my co-writer will mention it sooner or later. That's a clear sign to me to change it. At other times, like Annie Roboff said, you've got to be willing to fight for what you believe in about a song, but advisably, *after* you've thoroughly considered your collaborator's perspective. The ultimate professional goal collaborators share is to write a great song that gets cut; the more immediate creative goal is to write a song that you both/all love.

5. Be able to get together to write, or have a system of writing remotely that works for both/all of you.
To collaborate, you need to connect with other writers—whether in the flesh or across technological lines. Anything goes, as long as any two or more people are willing to make it work.

Cities. If you're in or near a city where a lot of music is being made, finding collaborators to work with locally should be fairly easy. The three main music hubs in America are New York, Los Angeles and Nashville, where most of the major record labels, music publishing companies and the three performing rights organizations (PROs), ASCAP, BMI and SESAC, have offices (see chapter nine). Consequently, many writers, producers and artists gather in these areas to be "where the action is." Many other cities—Miami, Atlanta, Detroit, Seattle, Philadelphia, Austin—have a strong music scene where artists and writers can find venues for performance, networking, collaboration, etc. Nashville is a great place to meet other writers. The country capital of the world for more than half a century, Nashville is also where all the gospel and Christian record companies have their headquarters. In addition, over the last few years a lot of pop writers have relocated to Nashville or at least spend a lot of time there. Nashville's Music Row is composed of several long streets lined with music publishers, record labels, management companies, studios, the PROs and other organizations that service artists, writers and publishers. Many of the music publishers have studios on their premises that are occupied daily by writers writing and recording new songs. I think there is a greater concentration of great writers in those few blocks on any given day than anywhere in the world!

You can also meet potential collaborators at songwriter "round-up" or "in-the-round" events that take place in most major music cities. If you're new in Nashville, I suggest going to the Bluebird Cafe on writers night. There are usually four to six truly great writers—some up-and-coming, some already successful and famous—and the audience will be of the same sort. In New York one of my favorite songwriter showcase and gathering places is the New York Songwriter's Circle at the Bitter End, hosted by songwriter Tina Shafer. Every other Monday night she gathers a versatile mix of great writing talent for an informal "writers in the round," which is usually attended by other writers, as well as artists, producers, publishing and record company people and the general public. A lot of successful collaborations have started from the Songwriter's Circle, and several singer-songwriters have secured record deals through the networking and exposure the Circle has provided.

The PROs and other organizations, such as the Songwriters Hall of Fame and the Songwriters Guild, also host a number of writers workshops, showcases, industry networking sessions, etc., in the major music communities, from which a lot of new collaborations and opportunities are born. (Check the event calendars on their Web sites.) People at these organizations have helped me from time to time find collaborators at a similar level of development and whose writing styles they thought would be a good match for mine. Sometimes all you need is a jump start, and once you're going you can't help but meet others who are going, too.

Smaller Communities. If you are not in a major music community, don't be discouraged. Music, like air, is everywhere, and music people will find each other wherever they are. Check out local music clubs, stores, high school or college music departments, church choirs or ads in local papers and music publications for possible collaborators and industry-sponsored events. Many clubs and other venues have event calendars you can easily access from a newspaper or Web site. A Web site I stumbled onto recently, Jeff Mallett's Songwriter Site (www.lyricist. com), contains an extensive list of songwriters in the United States and other countries as well, including the types of music they like to do and their E-mail addresses. You might also network with writers in other cities by getting referrals from music publishers, the PROs or other service organizations that represent and help writers. Almost every state has a songwriters association you can tap into for meeting other writers as well (again, check the Web).

Relocating. Probably the shortest route to finding collaborators and becoming a viable songwriter is to physically go where writers gather and music is being made. Bruce Burch of EMI Nashville and many other publishers I've talked to over the years insist that the best way to break into Nashville is to live there. Annie Roboff, a Nashville writer whose songs have been recorded by Faith Hill, Dixie Chicks, Trisha Yearwood and many others, was a transplant from Los Angeles. She said she realized she had to make the move when Los Angeles starting moving away from pop and toward rap and urban, because she didn't think she "could write rap as well as people who are living rap." Nashville opened everything up for Annie, she feels, because "I found myself surrounded by such brilliant writers that it helped me to connect whatever dots I wasn't connecting before." Annie has hit that magical time in a writer's career when what she loves doing most is what the the artists and record companies want, and ultimately the key for her was not so much in changing what she did but in going where somebody wanted to record what she wanted to write.

Foreign Flavors. Music has been making the world smaller and smaller over the last few years. The worldwide success of pop music coming out of London and Stockholm has spawned all kinds of collaborations between European and American artists, writers and producers. I was lucky enough to get in on this trend early on. While a lot of my friends were heading south to Nashville, I signed a subpublishing deal with BMG Sweden and started making trips to Scandinavia several times a year to work. I've found Sweden, home of Abba, Roxette and Robin, to be one of the most interesting music markets I've encountered. All kinds of music is being made there by talented artists and writers who are ready to break out into the world marketplace—and all some of them needed was English lyrics. With the help of Lars Karlsson and Magnus Osterwall of the BMG Sweden office, I developed ongoing collaborations with several major Swedish artists, some of whom eventually had releases in other parts of Europe and the United States as well. I've also had the opportunity to work with writer-producers who are connected with or co-owners of writing-production studios that have become major participators in the world pop market: Jorgen Elofsson, who works with BMG and Cheiron (Backstreet Boys, 'N Sync, Britney Spears, Celine Dion), which is a writing-production studio formed by Max Martin, Tom Talomaa and the late Denniz Pop; Anders Bagge at Murlyn Music (98°, Ace of Base, Ronan Keating/Boyzone, 702, etc.), who is partnered with Christian Wahlberg and Pelle Lidell; and Tommy Ekman, Christer Sandelin and Per Adebratt, owner-partners of Sprinkler (formerly Lemon Studios, producers of Ace of Base, Meja, Inner Circle, Aqua, etc.), a label and production studio working with Universal Records. Since then I've entered into additional subpublishing relationships with Warner-Chappell, Basart and Nichion, which has given me access to Holland, Japan, England and the rest of Europe for travel and collaborations all over the world. I take several overseas trips a year to write, but my collaborators and I have also worked out effective ways of co-writing when I'm not there. Either I E-mail or fax my collaborator(s) a complete lyric or lyric idea first and they write music to it, or they play me a melody over the phone, and I tape it, write the lyric and fax or E-mail it back. Then we get on the phone and go over phrasing, changes, etc., till we're happy with the song, and they go off and record it with the artist or demo singer. I'm also in the process of implementing computer software that will let me download music files via E-mail so I can write lyrics to full tracks.

Writing songs with somebody who's not in the same room is totally foreign to many writers. I can't argue against getting in a room with other writers and making magic together, but I also enjoy the cross-pollination of different cultures, musical styles and opportunities, as well as the flexibility of being able to work anywhere without leaving my house. Technology and the willingness to put yourself and your creativity in new contexts makes anything possible. A number of foreign writers who have had big hits in the U.S. now regularly travel here to work with American writers.

Andreas Carlsson, co-writer of Backstreet Boys' "I Want It That Way," Celine Dion's "That's the Way It Is," Britney Spears's "Born to Make You Happy," and collaborator with Max Martin and other writer-producers at Cheiron Studios in Stockholm. *I get inspiration from traveling, being in a different environment, listening to new music, working with all different types of people.*

Interestingly, the impact of foreign writers on the worldwide pop markets has also been felt in Nashville. Many Nashville writers have been increasingly influenced by European-American pop trends and encouraged to branch out by their own country/pop hybrid artists, such as Shania Twain, Faith Hill and the Dixie Chicks. And Nashville is going to harbor more and more writers like Michael Garvin, co-writer of Jennifer Lopez's "Waiting On Tonight," who lives and writes in Nashville but has a publishing deal in Germany with BMG.

6. Be willing to venture into new creative frontiers.

When alternative music became the new pop mainstream, the market got real slim for pop songwriters pitching songs. Alternative artists pretty much write songs by themselves, with their bands or close partners. Some songwriters, like an Eric Bazilian, have been lucky enough to hook up with some of those artists. Many other songwriters had to start looking for new venues to pitch songs to, which also meant learning to write in some new styles with new and different types of collaborators. One good example of this is my friend and sometimes collaborator Arnie Roman, who has expanded his success as a New York pop and R&B music writer into the Nashville scene as a country/pop lyric writer. I never would have imagined Arnie writing lyrics or venturing south of Baltimore. But within a short time of infiltrating Nashville's Music Row and writing with local writers, he had songs recorded by contemporary country artists Trisha Yearwood and Patty Loveless that went to the top of the country charts. And somewhere in there, he wrote a song with me that went Number One for artist Clay Crosse in Nashville's contemporary Christian market. I asked Arnie to tell me how it all happened.

Arnie Roman

Evolution. Fate. With no intention whatsoever, other than wanting to write something I love. I wrote a song called "To Have You Back Again" with Annie Roboff when she was in New York. I had brought the initial idea for the song to a couple of other writers before Annie, to no avail. But Annie responded immediately. When the song was received as well as it was there, it was an eye-opener for me. What was so gratifying was that, in terms

97

of my own input, it was a song that felt very true to my own voice, and it was a song I was very proud of. So suddenly, [part of] who I was, and what Nashville was about, were connected. Since then, I have continued to commute back and forth between New York and Nashville because the writing I do there in many ways continues to allow me to be my truest songwriter self— and Nashville is so song-centric, which as a songwriter is wonderful to be part of.

7. Be able or willing to find opportunities for getting your songs on records.

A factor that often goes through an experienced writer's head when considering a new collaboration is whether the other writer is connected to people and opportunities in the industry that might facilitate getting songs heard by record companies, producers and artists. If you know producers or artists who will listen to your songs, you've got a good "in." If you're working with a publisher, he will have a direct line to people needing songs, and hopefully he will shop your tunes and hook you into projects and collaborators. Of course, if the potential new collaborator is an artist with a record deal already, then all you have to do is write a great song that the producer and record company like as well.

So, to sum it up, I think finding the right match is at the heart a very subjective thing, and you'll know each time you find it—whether you're a writer who wants to work as part of a particular team or someone who works with many different writers. There have been many great songwriting teams (who also have collaborated successfully outside their teams), such as Holland, Dozier and Holland, John Lennon and Paul McCartney, Billy Steinberg and Tom Kelly, Terry Britten and Graham Lyle, Terry Lewis and Jimmy Jam, Elton John and Bernie Taupin, and so on. Some writer teams have been so well matched that they were married to each other, like Felice and Boudleaux Bryant, Cynthia Weil and Barry Mann, Carole King and Gerry Goffin, and Alan and Marilyn Bergman. But you don't have to be married, best friends or even like each other all the time—ultimately it'll come down to being able to write great songs together.

Warren Hill, contemporary jazz saxophone artist (five instrumental releases on RCA, 1999 Sire/Warner release "Shelter"), whose first vocal record, written and produced with his wife, Tamara, was released in 2000.

Being a saxophonist first and a vocalist second, melodies always come easier to me. To write a lyric, I have to be really inspired. Which incidentally is why most of my lyrics are about Tamara or Olivia [his daughter]. Before I started writing with Tamara, I struggled at writing lyrics. When we write together now it's like a well-oiled machine. Tamara usually comes up with a great hook and most of the lyric. I jump in and fill in the blanks, adding the harmony, expanding on melodies and the occasional lyric. Some of our best collaborations are usually written in one session.

Tamara Hill, writer-producer working primarily with her artist-husband, Warren Hill.

When I'm working with Warren, I usually come up with the entire hook—words and music. Then Warren, who is so incredible at filling in the blanks, proceeds to "glue" (imagine Dr. Evil) what I want to say into an incredible song. There is no exact formula. Sometimes we just sit down and bounce ideas off each other. It is great having a writing partner that complements you so well. It is also wonderful to have someone you love who inspires feelings that lead to lyrics—lyrics that are true and express feelings common to every human being in every walk of life. When you hit that nerve, when the whole world can relate— then you have a great song.

Cutting the Song Pie: How Multiple Writers Divvy Up the Song of Sevenpence

The statutory rate for the years 2000–2002 for songs released on CDs, cassettes or other audio media is 7.55¢ per unit (mechanical royalty), which will increase by about 0.50¢ every two years until it reaches 9.10¢ at 2006 and beyond. The standard percentages allotted to the two copyrightable components that define and protect a song—melody and lyrics—are 50 percent each. If you've written all the lyrics and the music, you get to keep 100 percent of the income and the copyright, unless you've assigned a part of your song(s) to a music publisher or other representative. If you've written the song with one or more other writers, you'll both/all share ownership of the song.

Most writers I know have the philosophy that the song should be divided equally by the number of collaborators. If there are two writers, and one writes the lyrics and the other the music, or they both do both, it's usually an easy 50/50. If there are three or more writers, the song is usually split equally— three ways would be 33 percent each, four ways 25 percent each and so on. I have found that writers generally like to be fair and even generous with each other. We don't want to count our own and each other's every word and note of contribution. It can ruin the flow to be worried that if you don't contribute enough words or melody in a song it will cost you points. In addition, writers who write together a lot often trade turns at writing more or less of a song each time they write so that eventually their respective contributions even out. In some circumstances, however, when a writer contributes significantly less to a song than the other writer(s), she will offer to take less of a share. However you handle song splits, doing the right thing by your peers will help to ensure that they'll keep being your peers.

When one of the writers is also the artist who will be recording the song, there are many ways a song can get written and split up. A lot depends on the strength of the artist's own vision and on his writing skills, track record and sometimes even psychology, as well as how established the writer is and his creative and professional priorities. Artists can be very protective of themselves and their projects, which is understandable in an industry that wants so much from them. Occasionally a major artist will want more of a split, because he is an instant vehicle for the song to be cut and therefore an opportunity for a lot of money to be earned for the writer. There are varying opinions about the fairness of this—some hold to the purity and integrity of the writing process, while others lean toward giving up a percentage to get a cut or be involved in a project, much like you would to a "songplugger" or publisher. If an artist is an inexperienced writer, then the song will probably be written mostly by the other "writer-writer(s)" in the room. If the artist has a good track record or a lot of potential, writers generally feel that the project is worthwhile, and the splits will likely be worked out to everybody's satisfaction—especially if they like working together. Whatever the situation, the chances of a song going on the artist's record are much greater if he has had some input.

There are as many ways to cut the pie as there are cooks in the kitchen, and it's important to have an agreement that is clearly understood and accepted by everyone. The earlier in the writing relationship an agreement can be established, the better, but if you are working in a new collaboration, you may not know what the extent of your contribution to the project will be until you get in there and start working together. Time and space are needed to play and create with all the different ingredients each person comes with. A writer may be brought into a project to "doctor" lyrics on a song and wind up co-writing a good portion of the record. Having heard many stories about song split questions or conflicts, as well as having experienced a couple myself, I would say simply this: sensitivity to each other's positions, and respecting and honoring each other's contributions, will go a long way to keep everyone highly creative and excited about working together.

Practice Exercises

1. Every day, take a few minutes to really listen to someone talk, and take notes. Try to capture a word, phrase or line that summarizes the main point of what she's trying to say, and use it to construct a title.

2. Get together with a kid and come up with an idea for a song together. Say your song is about the kid's dog, and the title is something like "I Got a Bone to Pick With That Mutt" or "My Doggone Dog Is Gone" or some other silly title. Trade off saying lines to each other to tell the story of the song, following the child's imagination and being open to crazy, nonsensical rhyme and reason.

3. If you're already working with a collaborator, explore how you can maximize your potential together in writing even better songs. If you don't have a collaborator yet, go find one, using some of the suggestions in this chapter.

Recommended Reading

The Songwriters Guide to Collaboration by Walter Carter.

7 Getting Yourself Ready to Write Lyrics

Let nothing happen in the sky or on the ground, in this world or that world, without your being in its happening.
  —Rumi (trans. Coleman Barks), *The Illuminated Rumi*

Even an immobile stone will respond to you if you approach with love. Call out, and talk to it.
  —Tetsuzan Shinagawa (ed. Mikio Shinagawa), *Talk to a Stone*

Go to the feelings that answer real questions.
  —Marshall Stewart Ball, *Kiss of God: The Wisdom of a Silent Child*

The most effective thing you can do in getting ready to write your own songs is to be alive to your own life. Live and feel subjectively, yet have some objective awareness of what you're doing. Second is to feel how your life connects with the lives of others and interweaves with and impacts their feelings, thoughts and doings. Third, start to see, hear, feel and think of everything as a potential song. Notice poignant, universal truths in the most everyday aspects of life, as well as the many different languages, colloquialisms and attitudes that can be used to describe the things we all think and feel and do over and over again. Fourth, put yourself regularly in the presence of situations and people that stimulate or share your dreams and goals.

John Bettis, writer of Madonna's "Crazy for You," Michael Jackson's "Human Nature," Whitney Houston's "One Moment in Time," Michael Peterson's "Let Me Love You One More Time," etc.

Inspiration, to breathe in, must become as ordinary as the other kind of breathing. It is a life work to keep oneself available to it. It is always there; it is our perception which fails to see and feel it. Take care of your body. Learn something completely new, and learn it well, at least once a year. Pick something you don't like and develop a taste for it. Love someone. Be loved. And write every day, if you can. A sentence will do.

Jenny Yates, writer of Garth Brooks's "Standing Outside the Fire," "The Red Strokes," etc., Kathy Mattea's "The Streets of Your Town," Dan Seals's "A Good Rain," Sammy Kershaw's "Harbor for a Lonely Heart," etc.

It's always a beautiful challenging puzzle. It's about being alive—looking for the aliveness in all things and situations. I think I find it most by looking out—then it leads me back in. If I get too stuck in my own world, I lose sight of all that's around me.

Taking Workshops and Courses

Most writers I know taught themselves to write songs by listening to other people's songs. Some, however, got a jump start with either formal music training or songwriting workshops. As I mentioned in chapter six, ASCAP, BMI, SESAC, the Songwriters Guild and other music organizations offer songwriting workshops for beginning as well as advanced writers in pop, R&B, film, theater and other genres. ASCAP also has a unique mentorship program for developing writers, organized by Marcie Drexler and songwriter Karen Manno, for one-on-one consults with experienced writers. I also suggest looking for local workshops or courses on the Internet by searching "songwriting," "songwriters associations" or "music education" and related topics. If you're interested in getting a formal degree in songwriting, check out Berklee College of Music in Boston, which is the first school in the country to offer a songwriting major. Pat Pattison, songwriter, teacher and author of *Writing Better Lyrics*, and Jon Aldrich developed Berklee's songwriting program—and if the thoroughness and enthusiasm of Pat's book is any indication of the quality of the curriculum, it should be very good.

Workshops and courses are great for networking with other writers and accelerating your knowledge of craft. But don't forget that it's also important to "study not knowing," as Beth Chapman said, to receive the inspiration and ideas that can give vibrancy to your well-crafted songs.

Studying Other People's Songs

It was partly my love of other people's songs that made me want to write my own. Listening to songs over time helped to give me a subconscious feel for how to write them. By actually studying songs, I learned how lyrics and music enhance each other through language styles, phrasing, rhythmic emphasis and emotional compatibility. I also learned about the structures that are commonly used, as well as ways to vary or break out of those structures and still have a great song.

Robert Sterling, co-writer of Point of Grace's "Jesus Will Still Be There," "Take Me Back," Luke Garrett's "I Have Seen the Light," Chris & Diane Machen's "Written in the Wind," "Worth the Wait," Margaret Bell's "Any Minute Now"

Early on, my inspiration tended to come from records and songs that I loved. I would mimic what I heard. Later, as I began to grow as a lyricist, I would write out of a genuine desire to say something I believed was important. Now, inspiration can come from just about anyplace. A lot of the time, it is born from something I read. A line from a book will jump off the page at me and say, "I'm a song. You better write me."

There are many great lyric writers whose lyrics you can study and learn from. I took a poll of about thirty successful, self-taught writers as to their favorite lyricists-gurus, and here are some who were named again and again: Bob Dylan, Bernie Taupin, Will Jennings, James Taylor, Paul Simon, Randy Newman, Gretchen Peters, Wayne Kirkpatrick, Paul Williams, John Bettis, Tom Douglas, Marty Panzer, Jimmy Webb, Joni Mitchell, David Southner, Hugh Prestwood, Alan and Marilyn Bergman, Shawn Colvin, Gary Scruggs, John Hiatt, George Green, Beth Nielsen Chapman, Billy Steinberg, Bruce Springsteen, Elvis Costello, Bono, Sting, Alanis Morissette and Sheryl Crow. These talented writers represent a wide range of styles, and I highly recommend checking out their work. If you access the PRO Web sites, you'll find the names of affiliated songwriters and at least partial listings of their recorded songs, which you can then track down on the actual records or other Web sites that reprint lyrics.

Although you can learn much about the craft of songwriting by checking out other people's songs, let the influence of great songs ultimately open, inspire and move you toward your own creativity. If you want to be a great writer, you can't end up as a parrot of someone else. Be your own person and write from your own passion, joy, pain and purpose. Below are some ways to explore and use your own life, as well as the world at large, as sources of inspiration and ideas.

Dowsing for Ideas

Keeping a Personal Journal

One of the best ways I know to practice observing and writing about life and love and your take on all of it is to keep a personal journal. I don't mean a daily chronicle of every event and happening, but rather the things, events, people, dreams, ideas, etc., that impact you and the how and why of your feelings about them. Many of my personal journals are full of scribbled beginnings of songs that emerged spontaneously while I was privately expressing how I felt about something. Being in touch with our lives and feelings is important to all of us, of course, but the lyric writer needs to be able to talk about it. If we're going to move others, we have to be able to be moved ourselves and to put those emotions into words. In fact, the need for emotional "co-identification" is probably the causal root of record sales. We need to connect with others who have had similar experiences, feelings and thoughts, while at the same time being inspired toward our own uniquenesses. Songs help us to remember who we are and what's important. And for the times we listen to forget, there are few things in the world like a song that can take us to the land of forgetting and still remind us why life is worth living and love worth risking a broken heart for.

Kathy Sommer, co-writer of Dana Dawson's "Have a Nice Life," Leslie Carter's "I Need to Hear It From You," Mamba's "All That's Missing," and songs and themes for various TV shows (Cartoon Network, etc.)

Writing helps me to feel emotionally connected to myself and others. I conjure inspiration by doing mindless *activities: walk-*

105

ing, showering, gardening, driving, riding public transportation, exercising—and mindful activities: "catching" phrases as they appear in conversation, keeping a journal, going on an artist date (courtesy of Julia Cameron's The Artist's Way). *What's happening? Lack of judgment, just expressing, enjoying the images and free association, stream of consciousness, being in the moment—inside the music. Magic ingredients: a safe environment, an ease with collaborators (not trying to prove myself or "please" others), strong creative, positive energy, having something to say—needing to get it out and express it.*

The Importance of the First "R."

If you've never written a word but you've been a reader, you already have one of the most important foundations you could have to be a writer. I've loved to read from the moment I learned how. Reading has given me options for ways to live, think, approach and process the world that are different from my own experience as well as confirming a lot of my own feeling, thinking and experience. In addition, reading has introduced me to endless variations of language and writing styles and triggered new "voices" in me to experiment within my own writing. Many interesting words, phrases, viewpoints, etc., in books, periodicals, poetry and other kinds of literature that resonated with me have been concocted into titles or story lines in many of my songs.

The three kinds of literature that have had the most impact on me as a lyric writer are poetry, short stories and what I call "magical" books. Poetry can teach about the beauty-in-brevity of language and metaphor as it seeks and plays with proposed truths in a small arena. Economy of language and an ability to get to the point/hook within a short time is vital to lyric writing. Some of the poets I return to again and again for inspiration are Emily Dickinson, W.B. Yeats, William Shakespeare, William Blake, William Carlos Williams, Walt Whitman, Rumi and various modern poets. If you write poetry, it's not a far stretch to become a lyric writer. While poetry and lyrics are both short vehicles for seeking and expressing particular truths, the primary difference between them involves form and function. Songs have choruses and are meant to be sung and grasped more or less immediately.

Poems only ocasionally have a refrain/repeating phrase of some kind and are meant to be read or recited aloud and ruminated upon. Modern poetry, in particular, seems to beg to be free of rhymes and traditional structure so it can venture unencumbered into intellectual/psychological/emotional unknowns. Lyrics, on the other hand, need a standardization of verses and rhyme schemes and hooky, repetitive choruses to help them quickly establish an accessible and memorable emotional known. But whenever I feel uninspired or unimaginative, reading poetry never fails to recharge and refresh my ideas and language.

Short stories give a sense of how character is portrayed and plots are introduced and developed within a brief format, and they can draw us into worlds of underlying meanings and ironies of relationship that make life—and songs—interesting. (This is particularly great for writing country songs.) Eudora Welty, Flannery O'Connor and Ray Bradbury are three short story writers who have given me numerous titles and ideas for songs.

Books I refer to as "magical" are those that seem to have a compassionately human yet otherworldly "larger-than-lifeness." Some of these, which I actually keep out on my coffee table, are *Winter's Tale* by Mark Helprin, *The Alchemist* by Paulo Coelho, *The Earthsea Trilogy* by Ursula Le Guin, *Perelandra* by C.S. Lewis, *Phantastes and Lilith* by George MacDonald, *The Holy Man* by Susan Trott, *The Little Prince* by Antoine de Saint-Exupery and—my latest favorites—the Harry Potter books. Like these works, songs are often little stages for conjuring magic out of thin air, reenacting real or imagined events and emotions and orchestrating resolutions that we sometimes wish for in real life. And like thin air, a song finds its way inside you, and the next thing you know you're breathing it, and it inspires and maybe even helps to transform real-life emotions and experiences.

Quotations, Common Phrases, Proverbs and Clichés. The really fun thing to do with a common phrase or cliché is to change it up with a clever twist of words or context so it has a fresher meaning—"She Got the Gold Mine, I Got the Shaft" or "On Earth as It Is in Texas." I once wrote a silly lyric using a play on the phrase "absence makes the heart grow fonder." Since it was a song about a woman warning her man to stay home more or else he'd find her gone one day, I changed the phrase

107

to "Absence Makes the Heart *Go Yonder*." This kind of wordplay is done a lot in country songs. Check out the *Dictionary of Proverbs in American Country Music Hits (1986–1996)* on the Internet (www.utas.edu.au/docs/flonta/DPbooks/FOLSOM/cmdictionary. html). This site has 284 entries for country songs based on common sayings, proverbs and clichés. Some of the writers used the exact phrase, others created clever variations. Here's an example of a listing:

WILL—Where there's a will there's a way.
267. Var./All.: *You can be the will that finds the way.*
Mary Chapin Carpenter. "Tender When I Want to Be." Writ. M.C. Carpenter. From: *Stones in the Road.* Columbia, 1994.

268. Var./All.: *If there's a will, love finds a way.*
Girls Next Door (Doris King, Cindy Nixon, Tammy Stephens, Diane Williams). "Love Will Get You Through Times of No Money." Writ. S. Lorber, T. Dubois, J. Silbar. From: *Girls Next Door.* MTM, 1986.

269. Var./All.: *The way in a small cafe found a will.*
Wynonna Judd. "She Is His Only Need." Writ. D. Loggins. From: *Wynonna.* Curb/MCA, 1992.

Periodicals and Current Events. These are great for drawing on unusual or poignant stories and situations. *People, Rolling Stone, Reader's Digest* and similar magazines are good sources here, as are newspapers—I even occasionally tap the tabloids for ideas if nobody's standing behind me in the grocery checkout line. You can also check out esoteric journals like *Parabola*, the Institute of Noetic Sciences' *Connections* or the *Utne Reader*, which can be rich sources for universal truths, themes and titles. I once wrote a lyric with the title "The Sound of Truth (From the Lips of a Liar)" that was triggered by Ray Bradbury's book *Something Wicked This Way Comes* and the Waco Davidian and Jim Jones incidents (and which was later set to music and recorded by artist Stefan Andersson).

Advertising

Other interesting and fun sources of ideas, believe it or not, are TV, print and radio advertisements. In fact, advertisers often borrow from existing songs for some of their influences, even when they're not using an actual song, which some would say has helped advertising to become more clever and entertaining. So, in coming full circle, maybe advertising can be a fun place for song ideas. Remember, though, that it's important to not out and out plagiarize. In addition, if your song or its title is too familiar or reminiscent of something current—especially an advertisement—an artist is likely to be turned off by it. Titles cannot be copyrighted, so legally you can use anyone else's title and they can use yours—it's just not considered in good taste to do it on purpose.

The Art of Conversation

Whether they're between you and others or those you "happen" to eavesdrop on, conversations are a great source of ideas. One night I was at dinner with my girlfriend, Carolyn, and we descended into talking cattily about some guy who'd been strung along by some girl who was "*obviously* using him." Carolyn said, "Well, if he was fool enough to bite that hook, let him dangle." She laughed as I went glassy-eyed and fumbled for a pen to write down what she said. I've also gotten ideas from conversations in which I was receiving or even giving helpful/inspirational advice. Other people's conversations are also a good source for ideas. Eavesdropping isn't hard to do when you live or spend time in a city like New York where hordes of people are on the street and in other public places all the time. I've gotten many ideas from bits of conversations I couldn't help but overhear on trains, buses and from passersby who said a word or phrase that hit my ear just as they walked by me.

Dreaming

The dreamworld—both the waking and sleeping kind—gives us the sense that life can be about much more than everyday living, and it has been a great source of ideas for me. I think of daydreaming as when the heart has slipped past the sentinels of the mind to play and wander and listen like a still-discovering child. It's a way of opening to receive inspiration, and it can come upon you when you're in the middle of doing anything. You can

109

also invite it by silence, stillness, walking alone in the woods or any number of nonpurposeful states of being. It may seem like a waste of time to a busy person with a never-ending list of things to get done and crunching deadlines, but the time you spend daydreaming can cut the time it takes to develop an idea by hours and days.

Nocturnal dreaming can be a fascinating source of ideas as well. At times I've lucidly dreamed pages of whole lyrics, knowing I was sleeping and must memorize as much as possible so I could wake myself up to write them down. Although I've never been able to bring an entire lyric from "the other side," I have sometimes been able to capture the essence, the title and as much as an entire verse or chorus. A couple of times when I was working intensely on a particular artist project, I dreamed that the artist came and told me what he wanted a song to be about and what metaphors to use. Uncannily, by the time he told me the same thing during waking hours, I had already written lyrics per his "dream instructions," and two of those songs wound up on his record! I've talked to composers who have dreamed incredible pieces of music that they tried to capture when they awoke. Although what they were able to retrieve was often only a shadow of their "dream compositions," they were sometimes able to retain the essence and a few key phrases that they could develop into something significant. The more you use information from your dreams, the more present, relevant and helpful your dreams can become to your work. It's as if the dreaming builds a bridge between your subconscious and your conscious awareness, so that over time your imagination develops a wider playing field and gives your writing another rich, endless source of inspiration.

Assembling a Lyric Writer's Tool Kit

As you start to write, and keep on doing it, you may favor certain tools that help you to think and write more easily, effectively, etc. The "tool kit" I've assembled over the years is composed of tangible, material tools and what I call "virtual," or inner, tools. This is what my writer's tool kit has evolved to contain.

Tangible Tools
- Laptop computer and portable printer
- Narrow-lined paper and roller-ball pens

- Rhyming dictionaries and thesaurus
- Metaphor, phrase, proverb and quotation dictionaries
- Favorite books of poetry and ongoing mind-bending, soul-searching, heart-opening fiction or nonfiction
- Title and idea notebook
- My favorite "reminder talisman"

"Virtual" Tools

- Willingness to venture into an unknown every day
- Courage to face a blank wall, again and again, and write on it
- Knowledge of craft without being limited by it
- Patience enough to take the time to learn new things
- Love enough to keep going no matter what
- Wisdom to know when to go in a different direction
- Humility to start over sometimes
- Faith that my songs will find their right places in the world, sooner or later

I'll admit right off that the tangible tools are the easiest to keep up with. I started out writing with paper (napkins, paper bags, toilet paper, margins of books, magazines and newspapers, graph paper, etc.) and pen. Now I usually write directly on a laptop computer because it can record my ideas quickly, and my first drafts tend to have less fat and more meat when I commit them to typed words right away. I take my computer to writing and studio sessions and on out-of-town writing trips. Sometimes I just take it from my office to my favorite mountaintop for a change of scenery. Everything else on my tangible tools list doesn't always accompany me now. In the beginning I didn't go anywhere without a rhyming dictionary and thesaurus, but I've used them less and less over time because I don't seem to need them to trigger ideas as much as I used to. Unless a song is a novelty, quirky, clever kind of song, the rhymes shouldn't sound contrived or draw too much attention to themselves. When you're really in tune with what you're writing about, you'll find that the rhymes come naturally from the meaning and the story line that's unfolding. Sometimes I even "hear" a particular rhyme that clues me to where the story—which seems to be taking on a life of its own—wants to go. That's when you know you've crossed the bridge from structure that feels like it confines your creativity to structure that begins to facilitate it. I still occasionally use the thesaurus in my computer, but rarely do I find what I'm looking for there, because I'm usually seeking a metaphor, not a synonym. And metaphors more often come from your database of experience, exposure and linguistic art—though sometimes a metaphor and common phrase dictionary can jog your thinking.

That brings us to the title and idea notebook, which stores fragments of thinking/receiving until they're ready to be developed. You won't remember a lot of the ideas that zoom into your head and heart any time of day or night, especially if they're seeds that need to germinate awhile, so I highly recommend your writing down *everything* that comes through. I guarantee that an occasional review of such a notebook will yield a gestating idea ready to come into fruition!

The last item in my tangible tool kit has been added in the last couple of years and is sort of the bridge that connects me to the virtual, or inner, part of my tool kit. My personal reminder talisman is a heart-shaped stone on the mountain path across the road from where I live. I had just returned from a long writing trip in Europe and was walking the mountain thinking about the writing I was doing and questioning the direction I was going in the music business. Suddenly, my eyes were drawn to a perfectly heart-shaped stone embedded in the earth directly in front of my feet. As I knelt down to touch it, I heard the words "follow your heart, and your feet will know where to go." That was my answer. I wanted to take the stone with me, but it was fixed on the path. It seemed fitting for it to remain there as a reminder whenever I venture into the "wilderness" of any unknown to let my heart be firmly entrenched as my pathfinder.

Despite nature's help, I have to admit that keeping my virtual tool kit in spit-shine shape has been impossible. I go in and out of willingness, courage, knowledge, patience, love, wisdom, humility and faith all the time. And it's often for the same reasons—disappointment and viewing rejection of a song as a judgment of its quality and/or my ability as a writer. Nothing can kill faith quicker than self-doubt, and nothing can take the joyful selflessness out of something done for love more than the fear of not being loved back. But, if your love for writing continues to be a hair greater than your fear of not being good enough, you can find your way back again and again. As

Paul Tillich said in *The Courage to Be*, "Courage is something you exercise not in the absence of fear, but *in spite of it*." Besides, after a while fear and doubt get tiresome and boring, and there's nothing like the next newly created song to bring you back into the flow of the ongoingness of creativity, life and brighter days.

Practice Exercises

1. Take a walk in nature every day, even if only for a few minutes. Find a spot to meditate, pray or simply talk out loud, and return to it every time you walk. If you live in a city, find a park to walk in and a favorite bench to sit on and let your mind wander for ten minutes to an hour daily.

2. Start or continue your title and idea notebook by coming up with one title or song idea every day:

   - Watch some TV talk shows with paper and pen in hand, and write down every funny, quirky, startling, moving thing you hear.

   - Browse magazines for song titles. First write down the original phrase or title you found, and next to it write a variation.

   - Listen for titles and ideas in every conversation you have or overhear, and write them down.

   - Make up a list of standard sayings or clichés, and next to each one write down a variation that gives it a fresher meaning.

   - Get hold of a *Billboard* magazine, or check out its Web site on the Internet. Look at the titles on the Hot 100 Singles chart and the Hot Country chart. Write down all those that seem to be twists on common sayings or metaphors that put a new coat of paint on an old picture. Write down any new titles that pop into your mind while you're doing this.

Recommended Reading

Poetry and Experience by Archibald MacLeish
Zen in the Art of Writing by Ray Bradbury

8 Ready, Set— Write!

If you do it, you can; if you don't, you can't.
—Tetsuzan Shinagawa (ed. Mikio Shinagawa), *Talk to a Stone*

You lay out a line of words. The line of words is a miner's pick, a wood-carver's gouge, a surgeon's probe. You wield it, and it digs a path you follow. Soon you find yourself deep in new territory. Is it a dead end, or have you located the real subject?
—Annie Dillard, *The Writing Life*

You that come to birth and bring the mysteries,
your voice thunder makes us very happy.
Roar, Lion of the Heart, and tear me open.
—Rumi (trans. Coleman Barks), *The Illuminated Rumi*

You don't have to know everything, or even anything, about being a writer to start writing. What you have to do is begin, and the writing itself will teach you. Over time you will organically do, read, study and notice things that will make you a better writer. The great thing about being a writer, as opposed to, say, an actor, is that you don't need a stage, an audience or a director to work. It's a standing come-as-you-are-at-any-given-moment invitation and the moment is always here waiting for you.

Eric Bazilian, artist and co-writer with the Hooters' "All You Zombies," "And We Danced," Joan Osborne's "One of Us," Ricky Martin's "Private Emotion," Des'ree's "God Only Knows," Jon Bon Jovi's "Ugly," etc.
   Songwriting is like fishing—sometimes you pull up a big 'un, and sometimes you come up empty-handed. But if you don't keep your pole in good shape and get on the boat every day

*you'll never catch anything. I realized early on that songwriting
for me was similar to studying math and physics . . . in that I
always had to work to the point of near-total frustration before
the Clear Light Experience kicked in and I Got It. Having had
some success at writing Good Ones has given me faith to persevere even if I feel like I'm totally Out There.*

As discussed in the chapter on collaboration, there are basically three ways
to write lyrics for a song: to a preexisting melody, lyrics first, or both more or
less simultaneously. As much as I love writing lyrics first, I've found that in
pop music there are many more music writers who like to write the music first
than those who like to write or are comfortable with writing music to existing
lyrics. And if you want to write in Nashville, most of the time you've got to
be able to sit in a room with people and write lyrics and music simultaneously.
It's fine to have a preference, especially if you write significantly better in a
particular way and are able to form compatible, successful collaborations.
Some, like lyric writer George Green, who prefers being off by himself to write
the lyrics first (see chapter six), have had a lot of success working primarily
one way. But as a developing writer, chances are you'll have a greater versatility
of opportunities if you can write all three ways.

Writing Lyrics to an Existing Melody

As I discussed in chapter four, you don't need to be able to write music in
order to write words for music. But you do need to be able to *hear* and *feel*
the emotion of the music and come up with words that capture that emotion
and fit the sounds and syllables of the melody. For me, the most important
consideration in writing to an existing melody is that something has already
been created, and it's my job to hear the feelings, sounds and words that
are implied by the music. As Eric Bazilian said, music and lyrics should be
the same song, and writers like Eric—who writes both music and lyrics—
usually write them somewhat simultaneously. Since I am primarily a lyric
writer, a lot of completed music tracks come my way for me to write lyrics
to. So, in a verse/chorus construction, this is how I approach writing lyrics
to an existing melody:

1. Feel what the music is saying emotionally and how. To get the feeling
of the music, I listen once or twice to however much of the melody and

track I've been provided (sometimes it's just one verse and chorus, which is enough to write the whole lyric). The first thing I do is determine the tempo—slow, mid or up. Then I determine the emotion of the song—sad, happy, romantic, introspective, poignant, questioning, yearning, defiant, aggressive, determined, attitudy, etc. I listen to the whole song once or twice. Soon the feeling of the music starts to conjure a sense of story, and I get flashes of images and sounds that evoke ideas and words that I start jotting down.

2. Come up with a good title and sketch the chorus. The next thing I usually do is identify the melodic hook and its placement so I can start listening for title words. As soon as I've got what feels like an authentic, singable (and hopefully interesting) title, I go about memorizing the rest of the chorus melodies so I can sketch out the lyrics for the chorus. The important thing about *memorizing* melody is that it becomes a syllabic "container" for the words to fall into without my having to think too much about structure so I can continue to be free to focus on the feeling.

3. Write the verses. When I think I've nailed the chorus, or most of it, I start focusing on the verse melodies. How the melody travels, the number of lyric lines (and musical bars), and how and where each melodic phrase resolves itself to pause or end one idea and continue or begin another are all guides for the same thing lyrically and help to determine rhyme scheme as well as changes in mood, tone and story information. This information becomes part of the memorization of the verse melodies so that, again, the *feeling* of the music helps the words to fall into the *form* of the music as if they were always there.

4. Write the bridge (if one is called for). The bridge is often the last section of a song to be written musically because it will come out of or go into an instrumental break before the last chorus, and until you've written the rest of the song you may not know how exactly to incorporate a bridge. If while I'm writing the verse and chorus lyrics I feel a bridge is called for, I go ahead and write a lyric sketch for it, which my collaborator and I can work out later with the music.

5. Construct the third chorus/outchorus. The third chorus often will get worked out with your collaborator when you decide exactly how you want to end the song. I usually have a feel for it when I'm writing the lyric, and if I don't intend to keep it identical to the first two choruses, I'll go ahead and sketch out some additional or alternate lines to try out when we deal with the end of the song.

While you're writing, don't forget to pay attention constantly to how well the lyrics sing the music—how the music and lyrics sound and feel together. Test them again and again by singing the lyrics out loud.

Writing the Lyrics First

As a lyric writer, I love to write the lyric first because I can do it whenever, however, and about whatever I want to. I can take into consideration a type of artist or just write what I feel and let it find its audience later. I'm creating something totally original, as opposed to matching words with the emotion and story of a preexisting melody. I've sometimes gotten comments from music writers that it's easy to write to my lyrics because they already seem like songs. What that means is that the structures of my lyrics usually match common melodic patterns. In addition, when I write regularly with certain writers, I try to offer them lyrics that fit into melodic patterns they seem to gravitate toward.

Remember when you're writing the lyrics first to vary the lengths and rhythms of lyric lines, especially between the different verse and chorus sections. Not having your lyrics too symmetrical, as discussed in chapter three, gives the music writer room to play with interesting rhythmic changes and hooky melodic phrasings. Finally, no matter how great your finished lyric seems to be when you give it to your collaborator, be willing to change some things to accommodate great musical ideas if necessary. On the other hand, if your collaborator writes something so totally foreign to what you feel the lyric calls for, you might offer to write a whole new lyric to the melody and take back your original lyric to do some other time.

Writing Music and Lyrics at the Same Time

I can't give you a particular process for this one; it will change with every person or group of people you write with. One thing I can suggest is to show up with some title or story ideas to bounce off your co-writer(s), and as I suggested in chapter six, be willing to consider and try out their ideas as well as being open to news ways of working. If you're writing both the music and lyrics by yourself, then you'll do it however you feel it, starting

117

from wherever the idea first pops into your consciousness and going where it leads you.

Rewriting

No matter how inspired your songs, don't be afraid to rewrite if something nags at you or your collaborator or if you suddenly come up with a whole different angle that makes the song more interesting or shoppable to a particular artist. Most writers will write and rewrite till they feel a song is great. Sometimes, however, you may not want to change a song at the request of an artist or record company unless you feel the suggested change makes the song better. You may have to make a choice between creative integrity and how much you want to have that song recorded. If you're lucky, the artist will go ahead and record it even if you don't make the changes.

Billy Steinberg

Rewriting is tough. I find it easier to write a new song than to rewrite an existing song. Tom Kelly and I did an effective job rewriting our song "Alone." We knew something was wrong with it in its original version. We rewrote the first line of the chorus—both the lyric and the melody—and that fixed it. It became a Number One song for Heart. That was fast and painless. In contrast, it took me the better part of a year to rewrite the lyrics for [the following] verse of "True Colors" when Tom and I decided that we needed to make the song more "universal" instead of describing one specific person.

Original Verse:
    You've got a long list
    With so many choices
    A ventriloquist
    With so many voices
    And your friends in high places
    Say where the pieces fit
    You've got too many faces
    In your makeup kit

Rewritten and Recorded Verse:
> You with the sad eyes
> Don't be discouraged
> Oh, I realize
> It's hard to find courage
> In a world full of people
> You can lose sight of it all
> And the darkness inside you
> Makes you feel so small

If you're rewriting for the artist, try to talk to the artist directly to find out exactly what changes he wants in the lyrics. With direct conversation, you might find out that it's really only a word or line or two that's creating the problem. On the other hand, I once labored for days over changing the entire story line of the lyric for an artist who finally admitted that the real problem with the song was that it was too "rangy" for her to sing as well as the demo singer had. Despite the occasional runaround, however, I don't really mind rewriting at someone's request—especially if the song maintains an integrity and there's a viable opportunity to get it recorded.

Writer's Block: What to Do When You Can't Think of What to Write

I don't think of ideas as getting blocked; I think of them as "gestating." Most writers have had times when we "can't" write and feel like, as Billy Steinberg describes it, "a dead piece of driftwood." I think if the words aren't rolling off your tongue, it's because they're still forming in your heart. The "block" is actually your own resistance to letting things be how and where they are in the moment. If you don't resist the time it takes, or get all knotted up in self-judgment, the words will come when they're ready. The consensus of the writers I asked about writer's block was that taking a break to recharge, refuel, remember and reconnect with what they care about always gets the flow going again. Here's what a few of them have to say about coping with having nothing to say.

Hugh Prestwood
I've always felt writer's block comes from two things. First is trying to write a "hit" instead of just pleasing yourself. You

begin to try to say what you think "they" want you to say rather than speaking from your heart and soul about what you want and need to say. The other factor is negativity. Earlier in my career I'd get stuck in a lyric and the doubts would flood in and that'd be the end of that. Now I just tell myself to relax and persevere. All my lyrics start out horrible, and slowly I improve and improve and improve.

Arnie Roman

Writer's block (although I don't really see it as a block) has come (1) when I'm depleted physically, emotionally or creatively, or (2) when I'm experiencing some sort of significant shift or growth within myself as a person, and I'm in that no-man's-land between what I'm familiar and bored with and don't want to dwell on anymore—and some new stance with myself, or new perspective on my life, and needing a new "voice" to express that with. I know what I don't want to say, but not what I want to say or how to say it because I'm not there yet. The solution seems to be to take a break for a day, or a week, or a couple of weeks—whatever it takes—until the "tank" is full . . . and I'm ready to write again.

Peter Zizzo

I believe that the more you write, the more you learn how to face the inevitable blocks that come along. The healthiest thing is to not bang your head against the wall. Go home. Laugh it off. We can't win every day, or even most days. Think about how many times Mark McGwire went to bat for those seventy home runs. Give yourself permission to stink sometimes. I actually find my bad stuff pretty funny. Some people might find my good stuff pretty funny too. The point is, always embrace and be grateful for the ability to try. Then go to a movie and come back later.

Beth Nielsen Chapman

I don't call it writer's block. It's sort of like you have to die to your identity as someone who can't do it. I try to separate the soul part of myself which is willing and capable of writing something

120

anytime. The spiritual part of ourselves does not interrupt, so if somebody's got the floor it's probably the intellect, the brain endlessly chatting—or some fear. What's really happening is that something's still germinating on a deeper level that hasn't been quite ready to be popped into my consciousness, so instead of being fearful I try to look at it like a dance and this is one of the parts of the dance where there's not a lot of movement going on. If I have a deadline, I just keep reapproaching it, with the same innocence and enthusiasm I started with, working with my self-trust and trusting that unknown and the length of time it takes.

Annie Roboff
A lot of the way I avoid writer's block is by being very open to what somebody else has to say, to see how much fun we can have musically that day—and not always having to be the one who has the idea. Sometimes I'll get tired of listening to what I'm creating, and I have to take some time off and listen and relax and see who's writing stuff that I really like. No one, myself included, wants to fall behind, but you can't write a great song every time—and sometimes it's other people's turns.

Tanya Leah
What's in the refrigerator?

What to Do With Your Completed Song

When you've finished writing your song, what you do with it will probably depend on many things. If you're a beginning writer, I suggest that you write another song, and then another and another. Give yourself time to learn. Don't spend a lot of time and money recording your first songs, because you will eventually want to rewrite some of them (if you don't put them on a shelf and move on) before committing them to tape. And don't rush out to play those first songs to every Tom, Dick and Harry in the music business. You don't want to wear out precious professional contacts too early in the game. Most pros are inundated by people trying to "make it," so chances are they've heard it all, or at least think they have, and they can be hard people to impress. Just keep writing, find a mentor or two whose

121

opinions and experience you respect and with whom you can risk showing your worst stuff. The ideal mentor will show you something worthwhile or salvageable in a piece of work even if the piece isn't working as a whole. A mentor should help you to see your strengths so you can build on them and your weaknesses so you can strengthen them. Value all opinions, even the ones that don't seem to make any sense, because there's usually something useful in any opinion—even if it's just to focus your own different opinion. Along those lines, try to not get discouraged or take someone's seemingly negative opinion too personally. Focus on being the best writer you can be rather than on getting stroked, and you'll become a better writer faster. If you're in a band and need to write songs to be able to perform, keep writing and test-driving them in front of your audiences. But realize that no matter how much your family and friends *love* your songs and think they should be on the radio, the music business often has its own mysterious agenda as to what the next "hot" sound will be—and quality of songs is not always a consideration.

An exception to this advice is if you're already an artist with a development or record deal and the people backing you have agreed to let you start writing some of your own material. In that case, they'll probably put you with experienced writers who will help you to develop your ideas, which can be a wonderful accelerated-learning situation for you, as Dave Novik of RCA said. If you don't have a record deal yet, but you're a very talented singer, then you may find experienced writers who want to be part of developing you as an artist and will be open to writing with you. Whatever your scenario, you *will* get better and better the more you write. And when you're "ready to stick a little toe into the big time," check out the next chapter.

Practice Exercises

If your schedule permits, and you're working on your own at the moment, I suggest doing one or more of the following exercises at least once a week. The first two will teach you to write lyrics to existing structures and melodies so that when you find a collaborator (see chapter six), you'll be ready to work with the music. The third, fourth and fifth exercises will give you a chance to form a lyric on your own without the guidelines or restrictions of a preexisting melody.

1. Pick a song that someone else has written and recorded, and put

new lyrics to it. If you have a hard time thinking up a different story for your lyric than the original, try writing the same story from a different perspective or person. For example, if the original song is a you're-doing-me-wrong song, write your lyric as the person that's done the wrong and try to justify yourself, admit it, apologize or whatever.

2. Pick a favorite classical, jazz, New Age or other instrumental (with no lyrics) song that has a strong melody and put lyrics to it. Construct your lyric syllables to match as closely as possible with the melodic syllables of the lead instrument.

3. Pick two print or TV advertisements with catchy slogans/titles and write a verse/chorus lyric for each. Use the slogans or some form of of them for titles, placing the title in the first line of the chorus in one song and on the last line of the chorus in the other.

4. Browse through *People*, *Reader's Digest* or some other magazine, find a story about someone who interests you and write a verse/chorus lyric about that person. If you're into writing wacky, humorous or sensational stuff, check out the *Star*, the *National Enquirer* or any of the other tabloids.

5. Write a lyric based on a standard saying or cliché, changing it slightly so it has a fresher meaning, a play on words or some other kind of twist.

9 Sticking a Little Toe Into the Big Time

No one knows for certain whether the vessel will sink or reach the harbor.
Just don't be one of those merchants who won't risk the ocean.
　　　　—Rumi (trans. Coleman Barks), *The Illuminated Rumi*

Before a dream is realized, the Soul of the World tests everything that was
learned along the way.
　　　　—Paulo Coelho, *The Alchemist*

Before you start knocking on doors, I suggest you do some research on your own to help you learn the who, where and how of shopping your songs. There are many books available that deal in depth with the business of music, but I think the best one to start with is *Songwriter's Market*, published by Writer's Digest and updated yearly. It contains current listings for songwriting organizations that help to develop and network songwriters, as well as listings of producers, publishers, managers, record companies, helpful music Internet sites, etc. You will also find in this comprehensive guide articles and information about some basics you'll need to know about as you progress in the music business:

- copyright law, terms and procedures
- collection of mechanical and performance royalties
- the roles of music publishing and publishers
- record company artist rosters and the A&R people who handle them
- the different genres of songs and artists
- production and management companies
- how to go about shopping your songs to artists, producers and record companies or finding someone who will
- film, TV and international music markets

For other books on every aspect of the music business you could possibly need to know or want to explore, *Songwriter's Market* suggests that you check out catalogs such as Music Books [(800) 265-8481], and online booksellers, such as amazon.com and barnesandnoble.com. Ditto for industry magazines that will keep you up to date with the latest and greatest artists, their songs and all the events and business that radiate and spin off around them. *Billboard*, the industry weekly that I mentioned in chapter two, is the magazine most songwriters and music business professionals consult to keep a bead on who's doing what, when and how well. You can also access it from the Internet (billboard.com). A number of private Web sites hosted by music aficionados, musicians, writers, etc., offer information and suggestions. I also suggest checking out the Web sites of the following music industry organizations that service the songwriting, music publishing and recording communities: for copyright law and procedures, the Copyright Society (www.csusa.org) and Kohn on Music Licensing (www.kohnmusic.com); for performance royalty and copyright information, song, songwriter and publisher information, as well as many other services and referrals to other organizations, ASCAP, BMI and SESAC (add ".com" to their names, e.g., BMI.com); for mechanical royalty collection and licensing, the Harry Fox Agency (www.nmpa.org/hfa.html); the National Academy of Recording Arts and Sciences (NARAS), the Grammy organizers (www.grammy.org); and the Recording Industry Association of America (RIAA), dealing with the realm of sound recordings (www.riaa.com) and related areas. Another Web site I highly recommend is the All Music Guide (www.allmusic.com).

Where to Go for Help From a Pro When You're Ready to Take That Step

As I mentioned in previous chapters, I found the PROs—which in the United States are ASCAP, BMI and SESAC—to be great information-gathering and networking sources, even before I was a member with songs to register. When you do get your first song on a record or in film or television, you will need to choose which organization you want to affiliate with in order to collect performance royalties from radio, TV, film, live concerts, etc. However, again, before you visit them in person, visit their Web sites to learn about the information, services and workshops they provide to potential and registered writer and publisher members. I've been a member of both ASCAP and BMI at different times and have found them to be very helpful at crucial points in my career (and I've heard some good things about SESAC from some of their writers as well). Since the music business is so much about connections and support, I suggest that you find somebody at one of these companies whom you and your music click with and go with that organization (you can only belong to one at any given time). It may not be easy to get a prompt response because these groups try so hard to help as many writers as they can, but keep trying. A personal referral wouldn't hurt. Taking a workshop or going to an industry event, public showcase or writers-in-the-round one of these organizations sponsors would be a good way to meet people. If you're too far away to visit in person, then use the telephone, E-mail, etc., until you find somebody who will listen to your music and make further referrals and recommendations as you progress.

Every country has a performing rights society (the United States is the only country that has more than one), but those groups usually do not get as involved in writer development as U.S. societies do. If you are a writer who does not live in the United States but you have a song released here, you are entitled to choose BMI, ASCAP or SESAC to collect performance royalties for you. If you want to visit the United States to work with writers here, whichever society you choose can be of great help in setting you up with collaborators and introducing you to industry professionals.

Other important organizations are the National Academy of Popular Music which sponsors the Songwriter's Hall of Fame songwriter services, workshops and showcases, and the Songwriter's Guild (www.songwriters.org), which has offices in New York, New Jersey, Nashville and Los Angeles. The Guild offers a whole slew of services to songwriters, i.e. song critiques and workshops, copyright information and services, publishing contract reviews and even song catalog administration.

Developing an ongoing relationship with a music publisher can be of tremendous help in advancing your career. If you sign an exclusive songwriting contract with a publisher, they will usually advance money to you during the term of your contract for living expenses, as well as for song demos, which could even include purchase of equipment if you're a writer-producer. Publishers also, ideally, help to develop your career by networking you with other writers, initiating opportunities for you to work on artist projects and shopping your songs to artists, record companies and producers.

126

I got my professional start as a staff writer with a music publisher. I was a neophyte in the business and had nothing to my credit except what the publisher saw as developable talent. Being signed to a publisher—having to turn in a certain number of songs each year, meeting new collaborators and having opportunities to work on specific projects—helped to give me credibility and taught me how to write for and maneuver in the marketplace. I've had and continue to have various publishing deals in either or both of the United States and Europe with BMG, Warner and others, and they've usually been instrumental, one way or another, in furthering my success.

It's getting harder these days, however, to get a publishing deal if you are solely a writer in the pop market. As EMI's Evan Lamberg and other publishers concur, the role of the publisher has evolved over the years from being writer- and song-centric to becoming more about singer-songwriters, developing them as artists and promoting their songs. According to Evan, out of each ten writers that EMI New York signs, "six or seven of them will be artist-writers, two or three will be writer-producers, and only one will be a pure songwriter." And maybe, a slim maybe, one will be a lyric writer. However, the picture changes in Nashville, which is more writer- and song-oriented—and a lot of writers start out with smaller, independent publishing companies that have fewer writers and therefore more time to help each writer make solid inroads into the business. However, because the smaller companies are independently financed or in joint ventures with larger publishers, they will often want to own a larger share of your publishing—which doesn't have to be a bad thing if you're a developing writer and they're getting you cuts.

Wherever you are and whatever kind of music you're doing, if you've already had some success and you bring it to the negotiating table for the publisher to participate in, you'll be a more interesting candidate and you'll be able to make a better deal. As Evan Lamberg agreed, "If someone has a hit and is available, everyone goes to chase it. That's the name of the game." And this is a good time to mention that before you ever sign any kind of contract or agreement, consult a music business attorney or other music professionals who can give you some advice about legalities and common practice, particularly in the context of where you are, how much success you've had, where you want to go, etc., in your career.

When you're ready to start approaching record companies with your songs, it's best to get a personal referral from someone in the business to see A&R people, who usually comb the marketplace for songs when an artist is getting ready to do a new record. For legal reasons, most of the companies don't accept unsolicited tapes. Dave Novik at RCA Records suggests having someone at one of the PROs make a referral call for you, or if you're an artist you might want to have an attorney or manager shop your tape. Every A&R person has a particular expertise and way of working with artists and writers. Here are some tips from RCA International A&R Director Vince DeGiorgio about how he likes to be approached:

- *Never think you are bigger than the song or the artist. It's about the sum of all of the parts.*
- *Bring me a lyric sheet, tell me what the song is about (even in a letter) and what the inspiration is.*
- *Give me one or two songs that you believe are your best. And that you would love if you were in my shoes.*
- *Never cop someone else's licks, tricks, chords or melodies and sell it off as original. We always catch that sort of stuff.*
- *Don't overdo it when you get some interest; don't pester the interested party. It makes a great song bad in a real hurry.*

I would add to that, be on time but be prepared to wait for the A&R person as long as you have to, if possible. Have some knowledge of the record company's artist roster. Ask the person you're meeting with what particular projects she is working on and what kind of songs she's looking for at that moment and make notes. If what she tells you changes your plans about what you were going to play, be prepared with clearly numbered and labeled DAT tapes or CDs so she can go quickly to the song selections. Remember that the more songs you play, the more you dilute the impact of each and fray the listener's attention. Unless the other party has allotted a lot of time to your meeting, which is rarely the case, try to play at most three songs, and tell her it's fine to play just a verse and chorus of each. If she really likes a song, she'll listen beyond that. Have lyric sheets accessible and offer them. Some people want to read the lyrics, but others prefer to focus initially on listening.

For suggestions in developing the *persistent* professionalism, as well as personal stamina, that you'll need to handle all the different reactions you'll get to your songs and to wade through the many attitudes and angles of the music business—with your passion and talent intact—read on.

10 The End of the Beginning—How to Keep Keeping On

In the sweat lodge, if you know how to listen, they can teach you a song that will help you survive whatever life has to offer. [It's called] endurance.
—Priscilla Cogan, *Winona's Web*

"Why do you like it so much?" [He answered], "Because I had to climb a mountain to get it."
—Annie Dillard, *The Writing Life*

He who stands on tiptoe doesn't stand firm. He who rushes ahead doesn't go far. He who tries to shine dims his own light. He who clings to his work creates nothing that endures. Just do your job, then let go.
—Lao-tzu (trans. Stephen Mitchell), *Tao Te Ching*

There are four things that will help you to keep at it once you've mingled your private world of passion and talent with the very public and exciting (though sometimes seemingly stone-hearted and deaf-eared) world of the music business: **purpose, perspective, perseverance** and **professionalism.** And if you take them in that order, each will lead you to the next and help fortify you against the forces that may threaten to defeat you at any turn. You will be a miraculous exception if you don't face a good amount of what most writers—no matter how successful they've become—have dealt with and continue to experience to some extent. Only an arsenal of inner fortification can withstand the barbs of rejection, disappointment, chain-yanking from broken promises, near misses and the time it takes for anything to happen—from getting a simple return phone call to having a song that's been on hold forever get cut, or not cut, at the last minute. Let's take a brief look at each of these stamina-building virtues as they apply to the world of songwriting.

Purpose

Keep remembering why you want to write. When rejection and disappointment make you feel untalented, unworthy or any of the other self-doubting *un* words that can totally *undo* you in a split second, remember this: Your right to write is your love/desire/calling to do it, not someone else's assessment of your writing on what just might be a "bad hair day" for him. If you keep banging your head on a wall that just won't budge, at some point you might want to ask yourself if what's on the other side of that wall is in line with your purpose and if you really do want it. While I was working on this chapter, songwriter Alex Forbes called and we got into a discussion about whether changing your purpose for the sole purpose of commercial success is satisfying when all is sung and done. Alex joked from her own experience of moving back and forth between commercial success and personal artistic projects, "Nah—as soon as you're willing to sell out, suddenly nobody's buying!" As good as over-the-moon success looks, sometimes you have to humbly accept that what you want to write may not be what *everybody* in the mass marketplace (as determined by the record companies) currently wants to hear. That's not to say, however, that you can't partake of different styles to get the *content* of your purpose across. And trends change. Your day may come, and if you find a way to keep coming back to what you love and do best, you'll be ready. And here comes another synchronicity to support what I've just said: As I was writing this very paragraph, I happened to pick up an old issue of *Billboard*. It fell open to an interview with hot country writer and ASCAP 1999 Songwriter of the Year, Phil Vassar, quoting him: "I was chasing my tail trying to write like everybody else wrote. Finally one day I just started writing songs the way I write songs. And all of a sudden, it started working." The trick is to have the commitment to keep going till you hit that stride.

Perspective

Keep your eye on the world and your heart in the work. Be at least somewhat on the lookout for what's going on in the music business and for what "they"—the artistic and commercial trendsetters, A&R "prophets" and other music biz seers and moguls—are looking for, predicting and planning. At the same time, to paraphrase Peter Zizzo, don't look over your shoulder so much that you lose sight of your own heart. The same heart that suffers the hits of rejection and disappointment is also your primary source of regenerative energy and longevity as a writer. Consider your purpose, and look frankly at yourself to see who and where you are or want to be in the music business world—what areas you need to strengthen and what niche might fit your particular talents and what you enjoy doing. As Ty Lacy said in the *2000 Songwriter's Market*, "Find what makes you unique. Then amplify that, perfect it—whatever makes people see that there's only one like you around. The industry is full of talented people. It's when you stand out that you're a success." I think Ty and Phil belong to the same club!

Perseverance

Keep doing what you love and loving what you do. Don't let anybody rain on your parade, at least not for too long. Let your love for what you do, mixed with the passion of purpose and a healthy dose of perspective, construct your perseverance umbrella—and whip that thing out whenever you see the first sign of sky falling. Sometimes an obstacle is something you must use all your energies and resources to go through, around or over to get to your destination—but at other times it's an indication that it's time to go in a different direction.

Professionalism

Keep your ears tuned and your mind on receive, and keep writing. Be willing to listen to people's opinions, and don't take them too personally whether they're negative *or* positive. There have been days when I scheduled several meetings with record companies to play the same batch of new songs. Sometimes there would be one song that everybody liked, but more often the very song one person was over the moon for would make absolutely no impact on another, and in fact I would get totally different reactions on every song. It's helpful to remember that other people's perspectives and agendas are not necessarily the same as yours or anyone else's at any given moment, and comments that may seem to come from left field may be central to their interests. Whatever they like or don't like about your song is being put forth from *their* particular context—which may be as immediate and narrow as that one uptempo song they're desperately looking for at 4:45 P.M. Friday before an emergency 5:00 meeting to decide on a still-missing first single that has to be recorded over the weekend to lead the pending immediate release of a hot act's new record—and their jobs are on the line. And *that's* the reason your midtempo ballad "drags" when they listen to it. Try listening not so much to what they say as what they're *trying* to say. For example, somebody might tell you that your three-and-a-half-minute song is too long, which is ridiculous. What he really means is that it *feels* too long. And that may be because the melody or arrangement lacks energy and excitement in the right places—or your song may be the one hundredth one he listened to that day. He may not be able to tell you what the real problem is, but if you don't get offended you'll be able to read between the "lies" and figure it out! Be respectful and gracious in attempting to extract something useful from whatever he's said.

When you meet a music business person with great ears who can articulate what she hears, listen and learn and be grateful. If a publisher, record company, producer or artist loves your song and is interested in publishing or recording it but wants some changes, be willing to hear his ideas and consider them. I wrote a song with Swedish writers Jorgen Elofsson and Tommy Ekman that had been on hold (an *option* to record) a couple of times for long periods without getting cut. When the last hold was released and I started shopping it around to record companies again, A&R people loved the song, but the musical style of the demo now wasn't current and hip enough to play to producers and artists. Michael Barackman of Arista and Vince DeGiorgio of RCA both strongly suggested we re-demo the song and gave some advice about the elements they thought were needed for it to be heard in the right way. We took their advice, and our publishers (BMG) got the new demo back to them, as well as to some other A&R people who hadn't heard it before. There was suddenly a lot of new interest in the song, and at this writing it's on hold for Faith Hill's next record, with a "backup hold" for another artist. Whether it will have been recorded or not by the time this book is released involves a level of miracles akin to acts of God and other forces of nature—but it's great to have come this far with some savvy A&R advice.

Professionalism is not only about how you interact with other people in your field; it's also how you navigate through your daily life as a professional writer. So when it comes to your own personal work ethic, have one. Be self-motivated, committed and disciplined, while at the same time keeping your heart open for the play of magic and the forming and mingling of ideas and timing. Whatever you need in order to write—whether it's a favorite pen, piano, proximity to the refrigerator or bathroom, a certain time of day or night, being alone or with certain others, a spiritual connection or lucky charm—embrace it, use it and enjoy it. If you let your art instruct and enhance your life, your life will in turn improve your art. Try not to torture yourself too much by overidentifying with being a writer and making commercial success synonymous with being a "good" or "happy" human being.

Annie Roboff
I believe in the daily work ethic. It allows me to consistently express wherever I'm at unconsciously, and that's very therapeutic for me. I think it's a privilege to be productive, and there's a responsibility that comes with that. Bill Cosby said in an interview once, "I just want to do one thing better every day than I did the day before." That had a huge impact on me, because you can actually end up being pretty good at some things after a while.

Admittedly, being able to quit your day job and earn a full-time living as a writer could absolutely and positively affect your quality of life on many levels. This is where purpose, perspective, perseverance and professionalism can give you the most mileage. Despite the increasing flux of young overnight sensations in the music business, the writers who have staying power are those who continue to work hard for their successes in the face of ever-changing trends, rejections and other challenges. And along the way, they've most likely developed some strong writing and business associations, as well as friendships, that have helped to advance their careers. However and with whomever you keep keeping on, keep coming back to the reason you probably started it all to begin with: because you love it! That next three to four minutes of song magic you create will take you at least one more step toward your dream. Or if it's your very lucky day, it'll catapult you leaps and bounds into the wonderland of a dream come true and change your life forever. *Anything* can happen!